Memorial Tributes

NATIONAL ACADEMY OF ENGINEERING

NATIONAL ACADEMY OF ENGINEERING
OF THE
UNITED STATES OF AMERICA

Memorial Tributes

Volume 10

NATIONAL ACADEMY PRESS
Washington, D.C. 2002

International Standard Book Number 0–309–08457-1

Additional copies of this publication are available from:

National Academy Press
2101 Constitution Avenue, N.W.
Box 285
Washington, D.C. 20055
800–624–6242 or 202–334–3313 (in the Washington Metropolitan Area)

B-467

Printed in the United States of America

CONTENTS

FOREWORD

THIS IS THE TENTH VOLUME in the series of *Memorial Tributes* compiled by the National Academy of Engineering as a personal remembrance of the lives and outstanding achievements of its members and foreign associates. These volumes are intended to stand as an enduring record of the many contributions of engineers and engineering to the benefit of humankind. In most cases, the authors of the tributes are contemporaries or colleagues who had personal knowledge of the interests and the engineering accomplishments of the deceased.

Through its members and foreign associates, the Academy carries out the responsibilities for which it was established in 1964. Under the charter of the National Academy of Sciences, the National Academy of Engineering was formed as a parallel organization of outstanding engineers. Members are elected on the basis of significant contributions to engineering theory and practice and to the literature of engineering or on the basis of demonstrated unusual accomplishments in the pioneering of new and developing fields of technology.

Together the National Academies share a responsibility to advise the federal government on matters of science and technology. The expertise and credibility that the National Academy of Engineering brings to that task stem directly from the abilities, interests, and achievements of our members and foreign associates, our colleagues and friends, whose special gifts we remember in these pages.

W. Dale Compton
Home Secretary

Memorial Tributes

NATIONAL ACADEMY OF ENGINEERING

Fredric W. Albaugh

FREDERIC W. ALBAUGH

1913–1999

BY ERSEL A. EVANS

FRED WAS BORN IN ALBIA, IOWA, received a B.A. degree in chemistry from the University of California, Los Angeles, in 1935; an M.S. degree in chemistry from the University of Michigan in 1938; and a Ph.D. in chemistry from the University of Michigan in 1941. He was a research chemist with Union Oil Company in Wilmington, California, from 1941 to 1943 and 1945 to 1947; and a highly respected research chemist with the Manhattan Project from 1944 to 1945. His wife, Edrey, was also with the Manhattan Project. He played a major role in the project and at the Hanford Plant with General Electric Company in developing a series of increasingly effective processes for separating plutonium from irradiated uranium fuel. For example, the waste generated per ton of irradiated fuel processed decreased thirty-fold over a period of only one decade as a result of the reprocessing developments for which Fred furnished much of the vision in addition to providing and developing world leadership in a brilliant, but self-effacing way. He also provided leadership in developing processes for extracting desired isotopes from high-level wastes and for vitrification of the wastes.

He played an important role in the formation of the Hanford Laboratories in 1956 to integrate all the research and development activities formerly spread across the Hanford site in separate organizations dealing with reactors, fuels, reprocessing, and other technical operations. He then envisioned and implemented a program for peaceful use of plutonium. With the help of many other organizations worldwide, particularly other U.S. laboratories such as those operated by Argonne National Laboratory at Idaho Falls, Idaho, processes were developed for a wide range of plutonium, uranium, and thorium ceramic, metal, and cermet fuels. These were successfully tested in many reactors in the United States and in other countries. Perhaps most important was the conception, building, operation, and decommissioning of the Plutonium Recycle Test Reactor. The reactor was built for $2.3 million less than the $15 million cost estimate while meeting the two-year schedule and operated from 1963 to 1968. This program was an important part of the foundation for a wide range of government and industrial activities, including both thermal and fast reactors, isotopic heat sources, nuclear rockets, and, perhaps most important, the present awesome commitment to disposal of large quantities of weapons materials. These activities have ranged from fundamental property measurements to urgent safeguards, transportation, and waste disposal problems.

In 1964 a management "revolution" occurred at Hanford, partly as a result of a joint diversification study by Albaugh and Paul Holstead of the Atomic Energy Commission (AEC). Operations originally managed by General Electric Company were opened to bids from other organizations. As a result, Battelle Memorial Institute assumed responsibility for operation of the laboratories as Pacific Northwest Laboratory (PNL—later, Pacific Northwest National Laboratory [PNNL]) or Battelle Northwest, with Sherwood Fawcett as the director. Battelle provided a major financial contribution, which resulted in building a series of facilities, starting with a $20 million Richland Research Complex. Ultimately, these expanded to include the Sequim Marine Sciences Center on the Washington coast and the Behavioral Science Center in Seattle, Washington. The long-time medical, environmental, and related studies of medical isotopes—their measurement, problems, and uses—survived these revolutions and continued as a world-class Life Sciences Center pioneered by Dr. William Bair as part of PNL.

Overlapping this major management change was another vision of Fred's—a large (400 megawatt) fast reactor test facility and supporting facilities, which could evaluate breeder reactor fuels and materials under a range of operating conditions. Responsibility for the actual construction and successful operation of this and other facilities was assumed by Westinghouse. The transfer of many Battelle employees to Westinghouse (with Battelle employment dropping from 2,300 to 1,300 mostly because of this change) left a new and potentially fatal problem for Battelle. But this was successfully met by another "revolution" in which Fred played a major role, ultimately as director of the Battelle Northwest Laboratory from 1967 to 1970. The challenge was to negotiate with the Atomic Energy Commission an "1831 Contract" which would provide permission for Battelle to do research and technology transfer to industrial and other organizations, as well as the AEC or other government organizations. Thanks to the dedication and statesmanship of both government and Battelle employees, the contract was successfully negotiated, and subsequent accomplishments from "a unique mix of science and application with a wide range of customers" have been remarkable. One of the first and most impressive of these was the launching of the Exxon Nuclear Fuel organization.

Ron Liikila, a long-time protégé recently summarized the decades-long evolution inspired and led by Fred Albaugh: "Through thirty years of change, researchers have invented dozens of technologies with a major impact on environmental restoration, energy conservation, health and national security. At critical points during those thirty years, PNNL also has reinvented itself, using its innovation and creativity to turn crisis into opportunity. That's the wave of the future." The recent construction and operation of the Environmental Molecular Sciences Laboratory as a collaborative, multidisciplinary research institute is a good example of this vision as well as a monument to the recently deceased PNNL Director Bill Wiley who made it happen.

Fred served as Battelle's corporate director for environment and energy programs from 1969 to 1970 and as consultant for other high-priority laboratory programs from 1970 until his retirement in 1983. He was a superb writer and was the author of many papers and patents, many of which are still classified. Government missions included Australia and Europe, and he was adviser to the U.S.–Canada Joint Program Heavy Water Reactors. He was active in community activities such as the Washington State Human Rights Commission and the Washington State University Advisory Group. He was a fellow of the American Nuclear Society and the American Institute of Chemists, and he was a member of the National Academy of Engineering, American Chemical Society, American Association for the Advancement of Science, Sigma Xi, Phi Lambda Upsilon, and Alpha Chi Sigma.

He is survived by his wife, Edrey Albaugh, and three children, their spouses, and four grandchildren: Jeffrey S. and Francine Albaugh of Portland, Oregon; James F. and Audrey Albaugh of Los Angeles, California; Jean A. and Gale McKnight of Anchorage, Alaska; grandchildren—Kestly and Stephen Albaugh and Lee and Lindsey McKnight, and brother, Marion D. Albaugh, of Olympia, Washington.

HARVEY O. BANKS

1910–1996

BY WILLIAM J. CARROLL

Harvey Oren Banks, a world-renowned civil engineer, noted for his work in water resources, died of leukemia at this home in Austin, Texas, on September 21, 1996. He worked as a state engineer and then director of the California Department of Water Resources from 1950 to 1960, and as an engineering consultant on worldwide water-related problems.

Harvey was born on March 29, 1910, in Chaumont, New York. His boyhood was spent on family farms in upstate New York. He received a B.S. degree in civil engineering (magna cum laude) from Syracuse University in 1930. Upon graduating from Syracuse, he went to Stanford University and spent three years (1930 to 1933) as an instructor and a graduate student in civil engineering and there received an M.S. degree in hydraulic and sanitary engineering in 1935. From 1934 to 1935 he worked for the city of Palo Alto, California, as a sanitary engineer and then served as a hydraulic engineer for the U.S. Soil Conservation Service from 1935 to 1938.

In 1938 Harvey started a long and distinguished career with the State of California Water Resources Division (later a department), interspersed with a few other assignments. From 1938 to 1942 he served as an assistant and then associate engineer with the division and then served in the military during World War II (1942 to 1945), serving in the Corps of Engineers. His overseas service was on Quadacanal. Upon leaving military service in 1945 as a major, he became a partner with Harold Conkling, Consulting Engineer, in Los Angeles. In 1950 he resumed his career with the state of California, serving as a supervisor and principal hydraulic engineer, then as assistant state engineer, and finally in 1955 and 1956 as state engineer. At this time, the new state of California Department of Water Resources was formed and Harvey became its first director. It was during this period that Harvey's visionary and creative talents were put to use in helping to formulate legislation and the diverse infrastructure that constitutes the California State Water Project. This gigantic system of dams, reservoirs, pumping stations, canals, and pipelines that transport water from northern California to the central and southern sections of California is one of the world's exemplary water supply and transportation systems, and a great part of its success can be attributed to Harvey's early leadership in its development.

In 1961 Harvey joined the consulting firm of Leeds, Hill, and Jewett, Inc., serving as president and chairman of the board until 1969, at which time he formed his own firm. In 1977 he merged his firm with the international engineering firm Camp Dresser and McKee, where he served as president of their Water Resources Division. In 1982 he retired from Camp Dresser and McKee, and again became an individual consulting engineer, and practiced as such for the remainder of his career.

In addition to his service to the state of California in the finalizing of the California Water Plan, Harvey served a wide array of clients, both nationally and internationally while in private practice. One of his major projects was for the Texas Water Development Board on formulating and implementing a long-range water plan for Texas. Another was serving as project director on the 6-State High Plains-Ogallala Aquifer Regional Resources Study (1978 to 1982) for the Economic Development Administration, U.S. Department of Commerce. There were many other projects and programs that he worked on throughout the world, including water resource feasibility studies and multipurpose water basin developments in such countries as Turkey, Bangladesh, Venezuela, Costa Rica, and Iran. Harvey also chaired state and federal panels throughout the United States and served on international commissions and committees on behalf of organizations such as the World Bank, the United Nations, and the U.S. Agency for International Development. He served as an expert witness before federal and state courts in a variety of cases involving various aspects of water resource control and management.

While accomplishing all of the above, Harvey published extensively on water resources management and water law. His papers were published in the journals and proceedings of the American Society of Civil Engineers (ASCE), the American Water Works Association, the Water Pollution Control Federation, the Institution of Civil Engineers of the United Kingdom, and the *California Law Review.*

Harvey was elected to the National Academy of Engineering in 1973. He also was an honorary member of both the American Society of Civil Engineers and the American Water Works Association, a diplomat of the American Academy of Environmental Engineers, a life member of the Water Environment Federation, a fellow of the American Consulting Engineers Council, and a regular member of a number of other organizations.

He received numerous awards, all recognizing his major contributions to the water resource field and to humanity. Examples are the 1976 Julian Hinds Award from ASCE for distinguished service in the planning, development, and management of water resources; the 1980 Icko Iben Award, American Water Resources Association, for promotion of multidisciplinary planning of water resources; the Royce J. Tipton Award, ASCE, for contributions to irrigation, 1973; and the Federal Land Banks 50th Anniversary Medal for outstanding contributions to agriculture.

In recognition of his outstanding work on the California Water Project, the first pumping plant on the California Aqueduct was named the Harvey O. Banks Delta Pumping Plant.

Harvey was preceded in death by his first wife, Mary Morgan Banks, and is survived by his second wife, Jean Ott Williams, and three sons from his first marriage, Robert, Philip, and Kimball.

Harvey Banks was a leader in the water resource field. His work has greatly benefited and improved the quality of life of many people around the world. For those of us who knew him, he was an inspirational icon of civil engineering, and we greatly miss him.

MELVIN L. BARON

1927–1997

BY JEREMY ISENBERG

MELVIN L. BARON, who died on March 5, 1997, at the age of seventy, was elected to the National Academy of Engineering (NAE) in 1978 "for contributions in structural mechanics, particularly in the fields of numerical analysis, ground shock and response of buried structures." He was widely recognized for his work in shock and vibration of immersed shells with application to ship and submarine design, as well as for original contributions to the design of blast-resistant "superhard" protective structures. Through his associations with Weidlinger Associates and Columbia University, he enjoyed a standing in both academic and consulting communities that was nearly unique in its time.

Mel Baron was fortunate to enter New York City College soon after World War II, when it was a major intellectual center, attracting students of the highest caliber to seek opportunity through free education. His intelligence and ambition brought him as a graduate student to Columbia University, then the nation's most prominent center for engineering mechanics, with a faculty that included Ray Mindlin, Hans Bleich, Fred Freudenthal, and Mario Salvadori, all of whom became members of the NAE. Mel's work with Bleich led to the first of many prizes, the Spirit of St. Louis Junior Award of the American Society of Mechanical Engineers (ASME). This was soon followed by the J. James Croes Medal and Walter L. Huber Research Prize of

15

the American Society of Civil Engineers (ASCE). He was later the recipient of the Nathan M. Newmark Medal and Arthur M. Wellington Award, also of ASCE, and served as the ASCE delegate to the U.S. National Committee on Theoretical and Applied Mechanics. He was also an elected fellow of ASME. Collaboration with Mario Salvadori on *Numerical Methods in Engineering*, an early classic textbook published in 1952, led to Mel's acquaintance with Paul Weidlinger, another future member of NAE, who had recently established a structural engineering consulting practice in New York. While a partner at Weidlinger Associates, Mel maintained connections with Columbia University, serving as adjunct professor and adviser. He received the Thomas Egelston Medal of the university's School of Engineering in 1983. He taught courses in integral transforms and complex variables there for more than thirty years.

Mel's partnership with Weidlinger lasted for forty-five years, until his death. As partner and board chairman of Weidlinger Associates, he established an applied mechanics group that, like himself, contributed academic research in applied mechanics and consulting services to a wide range of government agencies and civilian clients. He and his group were pioneers in applying numerical methods to simulate wave propagation effects from explosions. Throughout the Cold War era, he brought a high intellectual standard to the design and shock qualification of nuclear submarines and surface ships and to the design and testing of missile silos and antiballistic missile systems. He was frequently sought by colleagues and peers for advice and counsel on technical and policy matters both for his knowledge and for his unerring judgment. Of his many awards and honors, he was perhaps most gratified by the Department of Defense Exceptional Public Service Medal and Lifetime Achievement Award of the Defense Nuclear Agency. The citation for the latter award reads: "Dr. Baron, perhaps more than any other scientist, advocated experiments as the acid test of the theory of explosive effects (on structures). . . . He has played a prime role in shaping research programs addressing constitutive modeling of geologic materials, structure-media interaction, finite element modeling and the design and response of land and sea-based structures to weapons effects. Dr. Baron's singularly distinctive lifetime achievements reflect immense credit upon himself."

While a graduate student at Columbia University, Mel married Muriel Wicker who, until her death in 1993, was his constant companion and adviser. A graduate of Hunter College in biology, Muriel devoted herself to raising the couple's two daughters, Jaclyn and Susan, both of whom have engineering-based careers. Muriel was admired by Mel's friends for answering her husband's passion for work, stamp collecting, and paddleball with humor and untiring support. Mel treated his family to a wide variety of entertainment and culture through the years by sharing with them his enthusiasm for attending the theatre, ballet, and an occasional opera. Mel developed lasting friendships among those who shared in the many spheres of his life, including his neighbors in Riverdale, New York, where he lived for over thirty-five years; his paddleball partners; his colleagues and students at Columbia University; fellow fans of Columbia Lions and New York Giants football teams; and fellow stamp collectors. He had great love for dogs and, later in his life, for cats; he was particularly attached to Monroe, a large, tuxedo male cat who shared with his owner a good-natured tolerance and very social personality. In addition to two daughters and three grandchildren, he is survived by his second wife, Ruth.

Mel will be remembered by generations of Columbia students and scores of Weidlinger Associates' employees and numerous professional colleagues for the generous and caring spirit with which he nurtured their careers.

MILO C. BELL

1905–1998

WRITTEN BY ROY I. JACKSON
SUBMITTED BY THE NAE HOME SECRETARY

*"If it wasn't for salmon
there wouldn't be a clean river left in this State!"*
"Water that's good for salmon is good for people."

IN A PROFESSIONAL CAREER that spanned almost sixty years, Milo Bell, mechanical engineer, evolved and forged an outstanding career as a fisheries engineer. He worked throughout his long life to save the wild salmon runs of the Pacific Coast of North America from depletion and extinction caused by obstruction and other uses and abuses of the freshwater access routes and spawning streams and lakes vital to salmon's continued existence.

Milo Bell was born in Iowa on June 4, 1905. He came to the Pacific Northwest as a young man and received his degree in mechanical engineering from the University of Washington in 1930, as the Great Depression was beginning to spread its chill across the economy of the United States. Jobs were scarce, but Milo found employment helping to solve the problems of the salmon fisheries, which in the state of Washington, depended heavily on the wild salmon produced in the tributaries and lakes of the Columbia River and its 250,000 square-mile watershed. To understand his unique achievements in conserving wild salmon stocks, it will help to know something of their life history.

The five major salmon species of the genus *Oncorhynchus*, numbering hundreds of millions in total abundance, range both sides of the North Pacific Ocean and its tributaries from approximately the latitude of San Francisco and central Japan north to the Artic Ocean, including Alaska and north-flowing streams in Siberia. All Pacific salmon are anadromous, that is, all spawn in fresh water. Without exception, all are predestined to die after spawning once, giving their lives for progeny they will never see. All their offspring are programmed to migrate downstream to the sea sooner or later, in search of its vastly more abundant food supplies. There they remain, growing rapidly, until approaching sexual maturity impels their return to their home streams to spawn and die.

The salmon's requirement for access to freshwater streams and lakes for spawning conflicts with many other uses and users of the watersheds. Dams, diversions, waste disposal, and other pollution, natural hazards, and many other uses of the watersheds, all damage or destroy salmon runs. Since salmon cease feeding when leaving the sea for their parent streams and then migrate hundreds and even thousands of miles, delays or added stress can be deadly.

Major dams on the Columbia posed new obstacles to upstream migrant salmon enroute to their home streams. Their offspring, when headed downstream to the sea, met other hazards, including relatively still-water reservoirs, irrigation diversions, and turbines.

During the long era of dam building on the Columbia and its tributaries, Milo Bell, as chief engineer of the State of Washington Department of Fisheries, took the lead in conceiving and initiating the design and construction of many specialized structures to pass adult salmon safely upstream and their progeny downstream. He led the design and construction of rotary screens to prevent downstream-migrating young salmon from entering irrigation off-takes, which led only to death in farmers' fields. He designed and constructed hatcheries to produce young salmon in man-made environments where natural production was no longer feasible or adequate.

In 1940 a new phase of Milo's care began. In neighboring British Columbia, the Fraser River watershed of 90,000 square miles provided numerous spawning tributaries for great runs of spawning sockeye salmon, along with all the other anadromous species. Fraser River sockeye, inbound to spawn, were caught by fishermen of both Canada and the United States in their respective territorial waters. An international treaty creating the International Pacific Salmon Fisheries Commission (IPSFC) came into effect between Canada and the United States in 1937. Field investigations determined that a major obstacle to upstream migration of mature sockeye enroute to their parent tributaries to spawn existed at Hell's Gate, 130 miles above the mouth of the Fraser. Here, railway construction in 1913, notching into the wall of the 600-foot-deep granite canyon, had deposited masses of rock into the already constricted river, the eroded site of an ancient waterfall. Prompt action had been taken to remove the debris, but the passing of decades brought down more rock. This created a head of about nine feet over a short distance at certain stages, resulting in high velocities and excessively turbulent flow, which impeded or prevented the upstream passage of sockeye salmon. Because salmon do not feed enroute upstream and rely on their supply of stored energy for migration, delays can cause failure to complete their journeys or even death before spawning.

In about 1940 Milo Bell, first as a consultant and then as chief engineer, came to the IPFSC to lead the investigation, design, and construction of fishways at Hell's Gate to enable the free passage of sockeye at all critical stages of flow. Because of the restricted width of the river between bedrock outcrops, the river level could fluctuate as much as fifteen feet in a day. Dynamic model studies Bell organized at the Hydraulic Laboratories of the University of Washington led to the design of unique vertical-slot baffle "fishways" to be built into both steep and rocky banks of the turbulent river. Necessarily constructed during low water in harsh winter conditions during the years of the Second World War, the difficult construction was completed on schedule and within budget. Milo Bell returned to Seattle in 1951, having established himself as an outstanding innovator and leader in the specialized field of engineering solutions to the natural and man-made problems of migrating salmon.

In a career that continued for almost four more decades, he

dealt with almost every physical, engineering related problem of freshwater fisheries throughout the United States and Canada. In the same decades, Milo Bell produced designs and conducted model studies in search of solutions for fish-passage or protective facilities for migrant and resident fishes of every type and size. From 1940 to 1953 he was a special lecturer at the well-known College of Fisheries of the University of Washington in Seattle. His academic career at that college continued as he rose to the rank of professor in 1963 and to emeritus professor in 1975. He became a member of the National Academy of Engineering in 1968. He won the Eugene Baker Award of the Association of Conservation Engineers in 1969 and the Award of Excellence, Bioengineering Section, of the American Fisheries Society in 1984. In 1973 in recognition of his contributions to fisheries conservation, he was admitted as a fellow of the American Institute of Fisheries Research Biologists. His many publications included handbooks for problem solving and technical reports of research, design, and operational review.

Milo Bell's professional career of almost sixty years was single-purposed, working always to protect an important living natural resource from hazards arising from increasing human population and industry and the growing and competitive uses of our river systems. He was an environmentalist long before the concept became generic. His concern was always to hold the line, to minimize losses, to save brood stocks and gene pools. He knew that each separate stream population of each species developed its own characteristics and timing in response to the individual environmental characteristics and location of each parent stream.

To me, because I know it best, Milo Bell's outstanding achievement will always be the magnificent Fishway System at Hell's Gate, which has now functioned superbly for more than half a century. His innovative and unique design has become a prototype for solutions wherever comparable needs and problems exist. Self-adjusting and self-operating, requiring almost no maintenance, the design embodies no moving parts other than down-flowing water and upstream-driven salmon. Resisting the constant pounding force and energy of a major river in flood, they function for any salmon that needs assistance and are capable of safely passing a million salmon a day. Fishways so skillfully designed and placed that they offer all migrant salmon safe passage at the right time and place. A fitting monument to a great fisheries engineer.

Milo Bell's engineer son, Milo D. Bell, says it best: "The Hell's Gate Fishways were my father's pride and joy."

J. LEWIS BLACKBURN

1913–1997

BY WALTER A. ELMORE

J. LEWIS BLACKBURN, born in Kansas City on October 2, 1913, rose to dominance in a field of engineering that has nurtured many prominent leaders in the electric utility industry. He died on February 23, 1997. Lew treasured his roots in Missouri and never hesitated to cheerfully flaunt his "Show-Me" attitude. He received his electrical engineering degree at the University of Illinois, where he graduated with a B.S. degree. He started his professional career with the Westinghouse Electric Corporation in 1936 through the encouragement of one of the giants of the industry, W. A. Lewis, who had been understandably impressed by this brilliant young engineer at Illinois. His progress at the beginning was rather slow because of a speech impediment. Nothing could have driven him more unceasingly than this shortcoming. He was possessed with the desire to excel in this area where he seemed so unlikely to dominate. He succeeded beyond all expectations. Though still possessing a slight impediment, he went on to become one of the most respected and warmly received engineering lecturers of his time and taught tens of thousands of relaying specialists in their craft.

In 1952 Lew was made engineering supervisor in the Relay and Instrument Division of Westinghouse at Newark, New Jersey, and in 1955 he became engineering section manager of all high-speed relaying. His responsibilities included the develop-

ment of devices for transmission line protection capable of identifying the location of a short circuit and opening a giant circuit
breaker in 1/60th of a second. The success of this group of devices has not been surpassed by any modern-day apparatus, even
though we have all of the power of the microprocessor and its
associated technology at our disposal.

From 1969 through 1978, Lew served as consulting engineer
for the Relay-Instrument Division. In 1976 Lew and his staff developed an unrivaled textbook entitled *Applied Protective Relaying*, the dedication of which speaks volumes about his contribution to it. It states, "This book is dedicated to J. Lewis Blackburn,
without whose enthusiasm and persistence, it could not have
been written. Though the names of other authors appear on
some chapters, none exist without his imprint. His long-term
contribution to protective relaying goes far beyond this book, as
any of his thousands of students, colleagues, and friends all over
the world will attest."

His interest in the training and development of recent graduates went far beyond his promotion of and extensive involvement in the Westinghouse Protective Relaying Schools. He was
also, at times during his career, deeply involved in university-
promoted night schools. In addition to the obvious courses on
relaying, he also regularly taught a course on symmetrical components and systems analysis at Brooklyn Polytech, Stevens University, and Newark College of Engineering.

In 1978 he received the Fellow Award from the Institute of
Electrical and Electronics Engineers (IEEE). Also, in that year,
he received the Distinguished Service Award from the Power
System Relaying Committee of the Power Engineering Society
of the IEEE. The Outstanding Teaching Award was extended to
Lew by the Education Activities Board of IEEE in 1980. Also in
1980 he received the high honor of the Westinghouse Order of
Merit and the Lewis Blackburn Room was dedicated in his name
at the Coral Springs plant. He received the Centennial Medal
from the IEEE in 1984 for his long-term contributions to the
industry.

Lew Blackburn was active in the Power System Relaying Committee of Power Engineering Society/IEEE. He served ten years

as secretary of that body, then two years as vice-chairman, and, beginning in 1970, two years as chairman. With this exceptional record of service, he left a prominent mark on this committee.

During his very productive years at Westinghouse, Lew organized a series of lectures with members of his staff and presented them throughout the world. His students included hundreds of people from Brazil, the Far East, Venezuela, Canada, and Europe. His and his associates' notes for these schools formed the nucleus of what ultimately became the book *Applied Protective Relaying* and its successor, *Protective Relaying Theory and Applications,* which are accepted internationally as premier texts on the subject that he held so dear to his heart.

Another area into which Lew's enthusiasm took him was stamp collecting. To say that Lew was a stamp collector would be much like suggesting that Mozart wrote songs. Lew was a philatelist of the highest order. He was secretary of the Chinese Stamp Society and simultaneously president of the Polar Philatelists. His stamp collection was breathtaking!

Following his retirement, he wrote two more texts that have become classroom classics. The first in 1987 was simply titled *Protective Relaying.* It was complete with a set of problems that any professor would be proud to present to his students. The second in 1993 was another fundamental text entitled *Symmetrical Components for Power Systems Engineering,* which covered electrical concepts and problem solutions, not only relating specifically to the application of relays, but this time to the entire power system. He was encouraged to write more books, because of the clarity and simplicity he brought to complex subjects, but time did not permit. Lew left three devoted daughters and his beloved wife, Peggy, who followed him in death shortly after his passing.

JK Brimacombe

J. KEITH BRIMACOMBE

1943–1997

BY FRANK F. APLAN

J. (JAMES) KEITH BRIMACOMBE (NAE foreign associate elected in 1997), died suddenly of a heart attack on December 16, 1997, at Vancouver, British Columbia, Canada, at age fifty-four. He was president and chief executive officer of the newly established Canadian Foundation for Innovation and was on leave from the University of British Columbia (UBC), where he was Alcan Chair of Process Engineering and founding director of the Centre for Metallurgical Process Engineering.

Professor Brimacombe was born in Windsor, Nova Scotia, on December 7, 1943. He received his B.A.Sc. degree (with honors) in metallurgical engineering from UBC in 1966, a Ph.D. degree from Imperial College, University of London in 1970, and an honorary doctorate from the Colorado School of Mines in 1994. He served as a visiting professor at the Massachusetts Institute of Technology from 1992 to 1993 and was a professional engineer in British Columbia.

Few, if any, people on the North American continent can match his intense involvement and contributions to metallurgical societies. He was 1995 president of the Metallurgical Society of the Canadian Institute for Mining, Metallurgy, and Petroleum (CIM), 1993 president of the Minerals, Metals, and Materials Society (TMS/AIME), 1995 president of the Iron and Steel Society (ISS/AIME) and at the time of his death was president-elect-designate of the American Institute of Mining, Metallurgi-

cal, and Petroleum Engineers (AIME). He was also a member of
the Association of Professional Engineers of British Columbia,
the American Society for Metals (ASM) International, the Institute of Metals (Great Britain), the Iron and Steel Institute of
Japan, the Society of Mining, Metallurgy, and Exploration (SME/
AIME), and Sigma Xi. He was a member of both the Canadian
Academy of Engineering (fellow) and the U.S. National Academy of Engineering (foreign associate).

Dr. Brimacombe received twenty-eight major awards from Canadian, U.S., and overseas professional groups and nineteen
awards for best paper from professional engineering societies.
Among the many awards and distinctions he received were the
following:

- officer of the Order of Canada;
- fellow, Royal Society of Canada;
- fellow, Canadian Academy of Engineering;
- gold medal for science and engineering of the Natural
  Science and Engineering Research Council of Canada;
- Gold Medal of the British Columbia Science and
  Engineering Society;
- CIM fellow and Alcan Award;
- distinguished member of ISS, the John Chipman Award,
  the Charles H. Herty Jr. Award, and the Robert W. Hunt
  Award of ISS;
- TMS fellow, the Champion H. Mathewson Award, the
  Extraction and Processing Technology Award, and the
  Extraction and Processing Science Award;
- The Marcus A. Grossman Young Author Award and the
  Henry Marion Howe Medal of ASM International; and
- Williams Prize, Metals Society (Great Britain).

His award of the prestigious Canada Gold Medal for Science
and Engineering cited him as "one of the innovative giants of
20th century metallurgical process engineering and a role model
for young Canadian scientists and engineers."

In his obituary, officers of the Iron and Steel Society noted
that "Keith possessed a rare combination of intellect, energy and
engaging personality, which made him extremely popular and

effective as a leader," and "Keith's untimely passing is tragic and has robbed the iron and steel industry of one of its most brilliant and dynamic champions." His work and his reputation crossed many borders, especially between Canada and the United States.

Professor Brimacombe, at the time of his death, was one of the world's most outstanding process metallurgists. He excelled in teaching, educated more than sixty graduate students, and dedicated his career to developing the intellectual potential of those students he taught or whose research he directed. In his research he used mathematical models, together with laboratory and industrial measurements to understand complex process phenomena in both ferrous and nonferrous metallurgy. His studies led to world-recognized advances and cost savings in such diverse processes as the casting of metals and fused refractories, ladle refining of steel, calcination of limestone, roasting of ore concentrates, flash smelting of copper and zinc concentrates, and extrusion processes and microstructural development of steel and aluminum. The watchword of his research was the application of good science and engineering to the solution of practical problems, and he played an important role in building bridges between academia and industry. More than seventy-five metallurgical and allied firms sought out his advice, and his consulting activities allowed him to focus on real problems in need of a solution. He was a dynamic and visionary force in developing the outstanding materials processing program at UBC and founding the university's superb $21 million advanced materials and process engineering laboratory. This facility is certainly one of the finest of its kind at a North American university. In addition to more than 300 publications, he also disseminated his research results through short courses at UBC, at professional society meetings worldwide, and at many industrial sites. His annual course on the continuous casting of steel would typically attract over a hundred participants.

Even before his election to the National Academy of Engineering, Brimacombe had made important contributions to the National Materials Advisory Board of the National Research Council (1992 to 1997). He was an excellent committee member because his comments were always perceptive, well thought out, and based on reliable and timely information.

In a memorial to Keith Brimacombe, John Evans, chairman of the Canadian Foundation for Innovation noted that when Keith was approached to lead the newly established foundation, he offered to serve without hesitation, saying that he had received so much from Canada in his career that he welcomed the opportunity to give something back to help others. Evans also noted that Brimacombe cared deeply for those with whom he worked; to which we can add "Amen."

Since his death, the Brimacombe Foundation has been established in his honor at UBC to recognize young materials process engineers and to establish a Brimacombe Scholars Program for research in academia or in industry. In addition, a Brimacombe Memorial Symposium was held in Vancouver, on October 1–4, 2000, sponsored by those professional societies where he had previously served as president, MetSoc of CIM, ISS, and TMS. Nine foreign mining and metallurgical societies representing Australia, China (2), France, Germany, Great Britain, Hungary, Japan, and South Africa also served as conference cosponsors in tribute to Dr. Brimacombe.

Dr. Brimacombe is survived by his wife, Margaret; two daughters, Kathryn and Jane; his mother, Jean Scullion; and his sister, Margaret McKeowen.

Gordon S Brown

GORDON S. BROWN

1907–1996

WRITTEN BY J. FRANCIS REINTJES
SUBMITTED BY THE NAE HOME SECRETARY

GORDON STANLEY BROWN ranks high among the great contributors to engineering and engineering education in the twentieth century. Born in Australia in 1907, he enrolled as a junior at the Massachusetts Institute of Technology in 1929 after having received diplomas in mechanical, electrical, and civil engineering at what is now the Royal Melbourne Technical College in his native country. He received the S.B. degree in electrical engineering at MIT in 1931 and the Sc.D. degree in 1938, after which he was appointed assistant professor of electrical engineering at MIT. He spent his entire career at the institute, rising through the professorial ranks to full professor in 1946. He was honored in 1973 by his appointment as Institute Professor, a title reserved for only a few of the institute's most distinguished faculty members.

Dr. Brown's early academic efforts included the development of a course on servomechanisms, a newly emerging discipline within electrical engineering and a technology that would play an important role in the design of automatic fire-control systems during World War II and beyond. His book *Principles of Servomechanisms,* coauthored with Donald P. Campbell and published in 1948, was an outgrowth of his classroom subject. It was a seminal piece of work on linear feedback control and a widely used textbook for several years following the war.

Recognizing the future of feedback control and computers and the need for research in these fields, he founded MIT's Servomechanisms Laboratory in 1940. Through his leadership, several important projects emerged, including research on automatic fire-control systems, the Whirlwind computer project led by Professor Jay Forrester, the automatic control system for the Brookhaven nuclear reactor (the first peacetime nuclear reactor in the world), and the numerically controlled machine-tool project, a revolutionary technology that merged computers and servomechanisms with machine tools and redirected the future of the machine-tool industry. For his laboratory's work on numerical control, Dr. Brown shared, with William Pease and James McDonough, the 1970 Joseph Marie Jacquard Award of the Numerical Control Society, a professional society that was the direct outgrowth of Servo Lab's digital machine-tool research.

Dr. Brown will be remembered for his leadership in modernizing post World War II engineering education. When he became head of the electrical engineering department in 1952, major curriculum changes in his department's programs were already being planned, changes that would recognize new technologies that had emerged from the war effort and would have a major impact on the future of the profession. Dr. Brown immediately turned plans into action. His vision of postwar undergraduate engineering education was that it should emphasize engineering principles and be based on a solid foundation of science and mathematics. Engineering science rather than state-of-the-art engineering practice was his model for post World War II engineering education. He believed students' education should serve them in good stead for many years after graduation and an electrical science background was a prerequisite. Accordingly, he eliminated outmoded classroom subjects and replaced them with relevant ones; outdated academic laboratories were updated or eliminated if they no longer conformed to his model; and new textbooks were written not only to solidify internal changes but to assist other schools as they, too, began to cope with change.

Dr. Brown's appointment as dean of engineering in 1959 enabled him to extend his visionary ideas to other engineering disciplines both within and beyond MIT. The world was now his horizon. To expound his views, he published many papers on education, conferred with his friends in industry, and convened meetings of faculty members from other engineering schools to exchange ideas and to refine his thoughts. During the 1960s he catalyzed engineering-curriculum modernization abroad by establishing a faculty exchange program with the Technical University of Berlin and setting up interactions between MIT faculty members and faculty members at universities in India and Singapore.

Dr. Brown was a strong proponent of interdepartmental, interdisciplinary research that brings together faculty members from several departments and disciplines to work on problems of common interest in a research center. His success in developing several such centers at MIT was recognized to the extent that the concept of interdisciplinary research centers prevails at many research universities throughout the world.

By no means were Dr. Brown's activities confined to the ivory tower of academia. His outside activities included service to governmental, educational, and industrial organizations. During the war years, he was a consultant to the National Defense Research Council and the War Department. For these services he was awarded the President's Certificate of Merit and a certificate for Distinguished Service to Naval Ordnance Development. He was also a member of the board of overseers of Dartmouth College's Thayer School and a director-at-large of the Institute of Electrical and Electronics Engineers (IEEE) and its predecessor organization the Institute of Radio Engineers. Over the years, he was also a member of the boards of directors of several large corporations.

After his election to the National Academy of Engineering in 1965, Dr. Brown served as a member of its Committee on Public Engineering Policy.

During his career, Dr. Brown received many living tributes to his accomplishments. The citations that accompanied his honors and awards were like steppingstones to greatness, as each sought to capture the essence of his achievements. Early recognition came in 1952 when he received the American Society of

Engineering Education's (ASEE) George Westinghouse Award "for invaluable work in the development of the science of automatic control." Then came ASEE's Benjamin Garver Lamme Award for "his untiring efforts to advance professional education in engineering," and a similar citation for the Medal in Electrical Engineering Education from the American Institute of Electrical Engineers (AIEE). Accolades continued as the AIEE and the American Academy of Arts and Sciences elected him a fellow, and as he received honorary degrees from Purdue and Southern Methodist universities, Dartmouth College, Stevens Institute of Technology, and the Technical University of Denmark.

Dr. Brown's style as a leader in research and education was invariant. For each undertaking, he would put together a team of bright young faculty members, staff, and students who were eager to tackle tough new problems. After ensuring that they understood what the goal was, he would give them free rein to do the job. Along the way, he would be their mentor, strong supporter, and constructive critic, but most important, upon completion of the job, he would give them full credit for a job well done. It is little wonder, then, that his coworkers had deep respect and strong admiration for him.

An eternal optimist, Dr. Brown always looked for the one positive reason why something could be done, while ignoring the ninety-nine reasons why it could not. He was impatient with those who resisted change; in his mind those who chose to stand still had already taken two steps backward. His hallmark expression was: "the only steady state is the steady state of change."

His penchant for change continued even into retirement. Upon taking up retirement residence in Tucson, Arizona, he and his colleague Professor Forrester worked with the local school system to introduce a new kind of thinking in grades K–12 education. Dr. Brown negotiated a gift of classroom computers and funding to train teaching staff and to carry out experiments in the application of feedback and systems dynamics to physical, natural, and social systems. Building on this initial demonstration, many schools are now pioneering further advancements in system dynamics as a foundation for precollege education.

Gordon Brown died on August 23, 1996, a week short of his eighty-ninth birthday. He was a man who was deeply devoted to his family, to his wife, Jean, their son and daughter, and their grandchildren. He was their staunch supporter and wise counselor. They and all who knew Dr. Brown and were influenced by him will long remember him.

John D. Caplan

JOHN D. CAPLAN

1926–1998

WRITTEN BY JOHN BRUS
SUBMITTED BY THE NAE HOME SECRETARY

JOHN D. CAPLAN, the man who spearheaded the automotive industry's efforts that led to a drastic reduction of automotive hydrocarbon and carbon monoxide emissions during the 1960s and 1970s, died on April 27, 1998, in Royal Oak, Michigan. He was seventy-two.

Caplan was born on March 5, 1926, in Wieser, Idaho. During World War II he was involved in operations in the Pacific. He had just received his B.S. degree in chemical engineering from Oregon State University when he joined General Motors Research Laboratories on July 1, 1949, as a member of the college-graduate-in-training program. In September 1949 he was permanently assigned to the Fuels and Lubricants Department.

When the automobile's contribution to air pollution was recognized in the early 1950s, Caplan became involved in, and then directed, the technical programs that would define the problem and solve it. In just a few years, he became the leading expert in General Motors and the automotive industry on air pollution, and the principal influence in the formation of General Motors' policy with regard to the problem.

In addition to his technical capability and judgment, Caplan's leadership potential was recognized early, and he progressed rapidly through several promotions to become assistant department head in 1955. He completed requirements toward the M.S. degree in mechanical engineering, which Wayne State University awarded him in 1955. Later he attended the advanced management program in the Graduate School of Business Administration at Harvard University.

During the mid-to-late 1950s, Caplan directed GM's program that developed control systems for crankcase blowby gases and evaporative emissions. The General Motors Research Laboratories program discovered that a significant portion of the hydrocarbon emissions from a vehicle came from the crankcase breather, prompting internal venting to eliminate this source of emissions. Positive crankcase ventilation became standard equipment nationwide in 1962 and provided the first major reduction in automotive emissions.

By 1963 Caplan was viewed as an international authority on problems of air pollution from automotive engines and, in addition, General Motors named him to head the research laboratories' Fuels and Lubricants Department. In this position he guided research programs covering engine combustion, exhaust gas after-treatment and air pollution studies, and fuel studies. Related programs included the evaluation of engine oils, rear axle lubricants, refrigerator compressor oils, synthetic lubricants, transmission fluids, and chassis greases. The work involved research of a fundamental nature, as well as a program of product evaluation.

In this role, he directed the research program that elucidated the mechanism of photochemical smog, established the relationship of urban carbon monoxide concentrations to traffic density, and explained the sources of the various automotive pollutants. As part of this work, he supervised the design and installation of the automotive industry's first smog chamber, which could duplicate atmospheric photochemical reactions such as those typical of Los Angeles. He guided the development of gas chromatographic techniques and equipment for detecting, separating, and measuring minute concentrations of hydrocarbons in automotive exhaust gases, evaporative emissions, and smog chamber samples. These developments made it possible to conduct parts-per-million and parts-per-billion exhaust gas analysis for the first time.

Caplan had a great influence on the progress of both the automotive and petroleum industries in their joint efforts to optimize engine-fuel and engine-lubricant relationships. Operating in a key liaison position between these two huge industries, he directed an aggressive program to compel improvements in petroleum products used in automotive applications and to find ways to better use those products by hardware design changes. A considerable portion of the progress made in the performance and durability of automotive fuel and lubricant systems during those years must be attributed to Caplan's outstanding leadership. His direction helped ensure significant reductions in fuel system vapor lock, knock, and bearing and valve train wear problems.

In addition, Caplan negotiated with regulatory agencies of California and the federal government over emission standards and emission measuring procedures and techniques.

All these activities advanced General Motors' and the auto industry's cooperative work to progressively control automotive emissions. The collaborative effort began with 1961 model cars and resulted in an 80 percent reduction in hydrocarbons and 65 percent reduction in carbon monoxide by the time 1971 model cars rolled out. Caplan served as the automobile industry's spokesman on air pollution problems in the United States, Canada, and Great Britain.

Much of his outstanding contribution in the field of automotive emissions was summarized in his 1963 paper "Causes and Control of Automotive Emissions." For this, he received Britain's premier automobile engineering award in 1964, the Crompton-Lanchester Medal from the British Institution of Mechanical Engineers. Caplan also authored many other technical articles for engineering journals, including "Vapor-Locking Tendencies of Fuels—A Practical Approach" and "Smog Chemistry Points the Way to Rational Vehicle Emission Control."

In 1967, Caplan was appointed technical director, basic and applied sciences, for General Motors Research Laboratories. Just two years later, he was named executive director. He was interested and knowledgeable in a broad range of fields, which gave him the background necessary to direct a dozen research departments ranging from theoretical physics and transportation research to polymers and mechanical engineering. He demonstrated an ability to work well with technical and governmental leaders, a skill that served him well as chairman of the industry's key emission group, the Vehicle Combustion Products Committee of the Automobile Manufacturers Association.

Caplan was elected to the National Academy of Engineering in 1973, being cited for "Achievements in the definition, measurement, and control of motor vehicle pollutants." He was also a fellow of the American Association for the Advancement of Science, the American Institute of Chemical Engineers, and the Society of Automotive Engineers. He was a member of the American Chemical Society, the American Defense Preparedness Association, the American Management Association, the American Society for Testing and Materials, the Combustion Institute, and the Engineering Society of Detroit. He served as president of the Coordinating Research Council, as chairman of the Section on Industrial Science of the American Association for the Advancement of Science, as chairman of the Directors of Industrial Research, and as a member of the Advisory Council, Princeton University School of Engineering and Applied Science.

Caplan served on two advisory committees for the State of California Department of Health: the Automobile Emission Standards Advisory Committee and the Motor Vehicle Pollution Control Board Advisory Committee on Criteria and Testing. He worked with the U.S. Public Health Service Exhaust Gas Research Task Group and National Conference on Air Pollution Steering Committee, and served on the city of Detroit advisory committee on motor fuels and lubricants.

He was elected to the honor societies Tau Beta Pi (engineering), Sigma Tau (engineering), Phi Lambda Upsilon (chemistry), and Phi Kappa Phi (general). Caplan was also listed in *American Men and Women of Science, Who's Who in America,* and *Engineers of Distinction—A Who's Who in Engineering.*

Bill Agnew, a research executive who worked with him for many years, remembers him this way: "John had high respect for excellence and competence. On the other hand, he was a willful man who was intolerant of mediocre performance and aggressively attacked incompetence. As such, he was a leader who got things done, but was not universally appreciated. Both at work and in his personal life he wanted things right, and his ability to be right in his own decisions was almost uncanny. He was highly productive and had a stream of accomplishments, many of them carried forward through others, for which he often did not get credit. His editing of reports was sometimes cryptic with margin notes (e.g., 'nonsense') that left the author with no clue as to what was wrong or how to fix it; questioning him would usually get only a smile.

"Away from work John was a true gentleman, a fascinating conversationalist, and a man of many interests. He played an electric organ at home, as an amateur and only for his own plea- sure. He liked to socialize, and his sense of humor was subtle, sometimes to the point of being incomprehensible. He often left his sentences incomplete on the incorrect assumption that his audience knew where he was headed.

"John was a family man with great pride and love for his wife and children, and they had great love for him. They took many family vacations around the country, even when his children were grown. He appeared to be a dominant figure in the family, and that seemed to create great strength in the family ties. He was a big man in many respects."

Charles Amann, who joined the GM Research Laboratories the same year as Caplan and worked alongside him throughout his career, said, "John took on the field of automotive emissions when it was in its infancy. He had the inquisitive mind that marks a good researcher. Recognizing that there was more to that field than the chemistry in which he had been formally educated, he studied mechanical engineering nights at Wayne State Univer- sity, earning an M.S. degree. He took a course on internal com- bustion engines from me, and when the topic of fuels came up, I was uneasy, feeling that he should be up front doing the lec- ture. Needless to say, he was a top student. John moved into management fairly early in his career, but he never lost his feel for research and was a champion of those he judged to be com- petent in their fields."

Ernie Mazzatenta recalls: "For more than two decades, John

unfailingly accepted my invitations to guest lecture before the research engineers and scientists enrolled in my technical writing classes. Because of his insistence upon quality reporting of research projects, he always came in with useful information and advice aimed at helping them achieve this quality.

"He would devote about half of his visit to explaining precisely what he and other GM executives needed and expected to see in their technical reports. John was most emphatic about the need for an informative, rather than a descriptive, abstract. He also stressed the need to separate the details of experimental or test results from the conclusions that flowed from those results.

"John would devote the second half of his visit to answering questions. What impressed me most was his willingness—indeed, his eagerness—to remain in the classroom just as long as questions were being posed—never appearing rushed despite his demanding schedule. His great interest in nurturing quality reporting was not lost on anyone in that classroom."

After his retirement in 1987, Caplan continued to evaluate research proposals for the National Science Foundation and the U.S. Department of Commerce. He was a member of the Senior Men's Club of Birmingham, Michigan, and his condominium association. He enjoyed travel, golf, and working on his computer. His wife, Loris; daughters Barbara Russell, Carole Dolohanty, and Nancy Howell; five grandchildren; and his sister, Christine Medinger, survive him.

Wallace L. Chadwick

WALLACE L. CHADWICK

1897–1996

BY STEPHEN D. BECHTEL, JR.

WALLACE LACY CHADWICK, former vice-president of Southern California Edison Company and independent consultant to power companies and governmental organizations worldwide, died in Pomona, California, on June 5, 1996. He was ninety-eight years old.

"Chad" was born in Loring, Kansas, on December 4, 1897. However, he grew up in Redlands, California, graduating from high school there in 1916 and attending the University of Redlands from 1916 to 1920, with time out for service in the U.S. Army in 1918. As a distinguished alumnus, he was awarded an honorary doctor of engineering science degree from the university on Founder's Day, April 20, 1965, when he also delivered the Founder's Day address. A member of the university's board of trustees from 1937 to 1979, he served as board chairman for thirteen of those years.

Internationally known for his work in the fields of hydroelectric and thermal power, Chad's professional life spanned six and a half decades and included work on many of the major civil engineering projects of the twentieth century. His long, productive career began in 1922 when he joined the staff of Southern California Edison. During the next nine years, he served in various engineering and construction capacities, principally as division engineer for construction on the Big Creek hydroelectric development in San Joaquin, California. He also served for three

49

years as transmission engineer in Southern California Edison's general office.

Chad resigned from Southern California Edison in 1931 to become engineer, and later senior engineer, on the 242-mile Colorado River Aqueduct for the Metropolitan Water District of Southern California. When that project was nearing completion in 1937, he returned to Southern California Edison. There, he served successively as civil engineer, chief civil engineer, manager of the engineering department, and—for eleven years—as vice-president. In addition to general management, his vice-presidential responsibilities included direction of engineering and construction, atomic engineering planning and engineering, and research and development. Among the many projects for which he directed design and construction were the 92-megawatt Big Creek No. 4 hydro project; the 167-foot Vermillion Valley earthfill dam and spillways; and the 150-megawatt Mammoth Pool hydroelectric project, including a 406-foot earthfill dam, ungated spillway, and 3,370-megawatts in seven high-temperature, high-pressure steam electric power plants. His development of the first full application of digital computers for automatic control of large steam electric power plants earned him the Instrument Society of America's Philip T. Sprague Award in 1963. Chad directed planning, design, and construction of the San Onofre Nuclear Power Plant as well as nuclear research and development. He also performed research and development for seawater conversion for the Mandalay project and for improved air pollution controls. And, in 1962, the year of his retirement, he produced a report for Southern California Edison on the organization and practices of power systems in fourteen Western European countries.

However, Chad's mandatory retirement at age sixty-five was merely a springboard for twenty-five additional years as an engineering consultant, during which he served thirty-three clients on more than 100 projects in eight countries. The Bechtel group of companies, a primary client during these years, sought Chad's counsel on engineering and construction, contract administration, and project management issues in diverse fields, including rapid transit, water supply, and hydro and nuclear power.

During the 1960s, Chad lent his expertise to the joint venture of Parsons Brinckerhoff-Tutor-Bechtel in the analysis of engineering and construction problems associated with the underground subway station and tube of the new Bay Area Rapid Transit System. Bechtel also used his services on the Boston Massachusetts Redline Subway Extension for the Massachusetts Area Transportation Authority and for the Washington, D.C., Metro for the Washington Metropolitan Area Transit Authority. Bechtel water supply projects on which he consulted include the Skookumchuck earthfill dam and spillway for Pacific Power & Light and the Washington Water Power Company; the Pardee Dam for the East Bay Municipal Water District in the San Francisco Bay Area; and the Setif, Algeria, irrigation project. Chad also advised Bechtel on design and construction of the 5,300 MW Churchill Falls hydro development in Labrador and the 700 MW Manapouri hydro project in New Zealand. His nuclear power consultations for the company included the Midland, Michigan, Nuclear Plant; the Hanford, Washington, Fast Flux Test Facility; Washington Nuclear Power Projects 1, 2, and 4; and the South Texas Nuclear Plant. Chad also traveled to Saudi Arabia twenty-six times in ten years to fulfill his commitments to Bechtel as chairman of the Project Review Board for the massive Jubail Industrial Complex.

Chad's long list of clients included Southern California Edison Company, Consolidated Edison Company of New York, the State of California Department of Water Resources, Dames & Moore, and the U.S. Bureau of Reclamation. He was chairman of the board of engineering consultants for design and construction of the 10,282-megawatt James Bay hydro development in Northern Quebec, and—following his consultancy with Bechtel on the Churchill Falls project—became a long-time consultant to the Churchill Falls (Labrador) Corporation. He also prepared a special report on the adequacy of the engineering and foundation design of the Reza Shah Kabir Dam in Iran for Harza Engineering Company.

Chad was an active participant in several engineering societies and received wide recognition and many honors—among them, election to the National Academy of Engineering (NAE) in 1965. A registered civil engineer and a registered mechanical engineer in California, and a member of Tau Beta Pi and Chi Epsilon, he received the 75th Anniversary Award from the American Society of Mechanical Engineers in 1955. He was a fellow and long-time member of the American Society of Civil Engineers, which he served as president in 1964 to 1965, and which awarded him the Rickey Medal in 1971.

In 1969 Chad received the Golden Beaver Award from the Western United States Contractors for "Outstanding Achievement in Heavy Engineering Construction," and in 1978 he was selected by *Engineering News-Record* as "Construction's Man of the Year." Named an honorary member of the American Society of Mechanical Engineers in 1979, Chad was also a fellow of the Institute of Electrical and Electronics Engineers and a member of the American Concrete Institute and the United States Committee of the International Commission on Large Dams.

Indicative of Chad's stature in the engineering community, he was appointed in June 1976 to head a six-member panel of experts recommended by the NAE, the National Academy of Sciences, and other organizations to determine the cause of the disastrous collapse of the 307-foot-high Teton Dam. The dam had collapsed while its reservoir was being filled for the first time, killing eleven persons and causing $1 billion in property damage. The resulting 400-page report faulted the U.S. Bureau of Reclamation for selecting an "unfortunate" design and failing to heed normal safety precautions.

Government agencies and companies worldwide continued for many years to value Chad's vast knowledge and experience. But organizations closer to home also benefited from his energy and wisdom: Chad served for eight years as a member of the San Marino City Council; twenty-three years on the Water and Power Committee of the Los Angeles Chamber of Commerce; and twenty years on the Advisory Committee on Saline Water Conversion for the Water Resources Center at the University of California.

Chad's wife of seventy-one years and former University of Redlands classmate, Beulah Dye Chadwick, died in 1992. After his death in 1996, the Huntington Library in Pasadena, California, requested—and received—from Chad's family his papers for inclusion in a new collection on the history of civil engineering. The collection, established by Trent Dames of Dames & Moore as the fund for the Heritage of Civil Engineering, ensures a permanent record of the integrity and lifelong achievements of Wallace Lacy Chadwick.

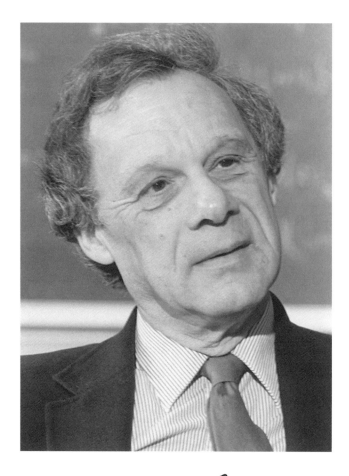

Julian D. Cole

JULIAN D. COLE

1925–1999

BY MARSHALL P. TULIN AND RUSSELL R. O'NEILL

The engineering community, and particularly aeronautics, suffered a great loss with the death of Julian David Cole on April 17, 1999, at the age of seventy-four. He was well known throughout the world and highly admired for his mathematical analyses of high-speed flows in aerodynamics, for his pioneering work in the development of modern perturbation methods and their application to complex nonlinear problems in engineering, for his books on these subjects, as an industrial consultant, and as an influential teacher. He was elected to the National Academy of Engineering in 1976 and to the National Academy of Sciences in the same year.

Julian was born in Brooklyn, New York, on April 2, 1925. He received his B.S. degree in engineering from Cornell University and his Ph.D. degree from the California Institute of Technology, where he worked with Hans Liepmann. During his career he was a faculty member at Caltech, scientific liaison officer in London for the Office of Naval Research, a faculty scholar at Boeing, a faculty member and department chair at the University of California at Los Angeles, and a chaired professor at Rensselaer Polytechnic Institute. He was a fellow of the American Physical Society, the American Institute of Aeronautics and Astronautics, and the American Academy of Arts and Sciences. Among other awards he received the Theodore von Kármán Prize

(Society for Industrial and Applied Mathematics), the Award for Meritorious Civilian Service (U.S. Air Force), the Fluid Dynamics Award (American Institute of Aeronautics and Astronautics), and the National Academy of Sciences Award in Applied Mathematics and Numerical Analysis.

Julian began his career at the Guggenheim Aeronautical Laboratories in the mid-1940s, just at the time when an assault on the sound barrier had become a subject of high national priority and when there existed a great and recognized need for the development of nonlinear aerodynamics, especially in the transonic regime. Unfortunately, transonic flows were poorly understood from a fundamental point of view, impossible to calculate, and difficult to study experimentally. Quite remarkably, in his first technical paper in 1948 (with Hans Liepmann), Cole actually foresaw the possibility of shock-free transonic airfoils, in whose development he was later to play a major role. The practical development of transonic wings for advanced transport aircraft, based on this idea, eventually depended on the availability of a suitable calculating method. Great mathematical difficulties stood in the way of this development. The difficulties arose from the nonlinear nature of the flow in this regime, with the matching of the flow about the lifting wing with the far field, and with the development of a stable method of calculation that automatically incorporates shock waves. The first and essential breakthrough in this development was accomplished by Cole while working with Earll Murman at Boeing from 1968 to 1969. Their work on transonic foil theory, published in 1971, showed the way and provided the inspiration for most future transonic calculations of aircraft components and led to important improvements in aircraft efficiency.

His influence in aerodynamics extends far beyond the preceding specific work. From his beginning in 1948, he went on to illuminate the entire field of transonics through a long sequence of research papers and the influential book *Transonic Aerodynamics*, 1986, (with Pam Cook). His work was always driven by applications and characterized by a fierce determination to find correct solutions without compromise and despite mathematical difficulties. He influenced and dominated the subject of transonic aerodynamic theory for fifty years. He had a similar influence in the field of hypersonic aerodynamics, beginning in the mid-1940s. This field grew with a focus on warhead problems and then returned to the fore with national interest in the Aerospace Plane. Here his early theory of optimum wings based on a "waverider" concept is very important.

The need to cope with nonlinear phenomena, while urgent and highly visible in aeronautics, existed then throughout engineering and science. A general recognition of this need and response to it began slowly in the 1940s but accelerated continuously and continues with great vigor to this day. The effect on engineering practice has been profound, and especially after the advent of the computer. In this fifty-year development, Julian Cole played a leading and decisive role. It began again early in his career with the development, together with others in a small group at Caltech around the aerodynamicist-mathematician Paco Lagerstrom, of new and innovative general methods of analysis of nonlinear problems. Cole continued persistently in this direction for fifty years, both in the form of general developments, and in special applications of many kinds. His methods have been propogated through many papers and several books: *Perturbation Methods in Applied Mathematics*, first edition 1968, second edition (with J. Kevorkian) 1980; *Similarity Methods for Differential Equations*, 1974 (with G. Bluman); and *Multiple Scale and Singular Perturbation Methods*, 1996 (with J. Kevorkian). The methods developed in these books have found application to nonlinear problems throughout engineering and have provided inspiration and a springboard for a whole generation of engineers faced with the analysis of nonlinear problems in all fields.

Throughout his career, and with considerable acclaim from the mathematical community, Cole persisted in his interest to find a solution to difficult engineering problems, not only in aeronautics, but also in fields as disparate as the mechanics of the cochlea in the ear, and in the effect of radiation in the generation of holes and electrons in semiconductors. Throughout his career he sought to present results of interest directly to his peers at engineering conferences. And of course he persisted, with devotion to the education of engineers, in bringing to that task and to the university around him a special integrity and wisdom.

He served as an example for all of us engaged in engineering research and education, and not least of all for his wholehearted attention to real engineering problems and to the needs of industry and for bringing his solutions and the means for finding solutions to real practitioners. He will be much missed.

A scientific biography of Julian Cole and a list of his papers and of his many Ph.D. students may be found in the book *Mathematics Is for Solving Problems* (Society for Industrial and Applied Mathematics, 1996) which was published on the occasion of his seventieth birthday.

Alfred R Cooper

ALFRED R. COOPER, JR.

1924–1996

BY WILLIAM R. PRINDLE

ALFRED R. COOPER, JR., emeritus professor of ceramics at Case Western Reserve University, died on December 13, 1996.

Al was born on January 1, 1924, in New York City and grew up in the nearby community of White Plains. His mother, of German descent, served as a homemaker, and his father, of Irish ancestry, was a self-employed glove salesman who traveled throughout the New York and New England area. A grandmother and other relatives lived in the neighborhood, and from all accounts Al and his sister, Betty, enjoyed a happy childhood. Al was interested in sports, and beyond the usual schoolyard sports he learned to play tennis and golf, and when he was old enough, he would occasionally accompany his father on his sales trips, where he had the opportunity to play on many New England golf courses.

He was a good student with a great curiosity about everything and everybody around him, a trait that remained with him all his life. Al had a well-rounded high school career, playing in the band and also playing basketball, but he demonstrated a particular gift for mathematics and science, making perfect scores on the New York State Regent's exams. After he graduated from White Plains High School, he entered Alfred University in 1941 as an engineering student, majoring in glass technology. As World War II progressed, he became increasingly caught up in the conflict, and in 1943 joined the U.S. Navy, obtaining a commission and serving as an officer on a destroyer in the Pacific. Al was discharged in 1946 and returned to Alfred University, where he resumed his studies.

Not all of his time was devoted to class work, however, and Al, who was tall and quick, became a major player on the university's basketball team. One account of the time described Al as "a bright light in an otherwise dismal season." He also read widely and developed a lifelong love of poetry.

Upon obtaining his B.S. degree in glass technology in 1948, Al took a position as a group leader in the RCA Cathode Ray Tube Production plant in Lancaster, Pennsylvania. In the four years that he worked at RCA, he learned a great deal about the behavior and problems of glass tank melting furnaces, and this knowledge helped to qualify him for his next position, in 1952, as manager of laboratories for the Hartford Empire Division of the Emhart Corporation. In his new job Al traveled widely throughout the country, working as a troubleshooter solving glass composition and melting problems for a variety of glass companies. He became well known in the glass industry, was an articulate participant in technical meetings, and served on various industry testing committees.

Nevertheless, in 1956, he decided to seek an advanced degree to learn, as he put it to a friend, more about the physics and chemistry that lay behind the phenomena that he observed in his glass plant problem solving. He had four children at the time, so this was a major change in his family's circumstances. In 1960 he received a doctor of science degree at the Massachusetts Institute of Technology and became an assistant professor of ceramics at MIT, and later (1963) an associate professor.

In 1965 Al left MIT and founded the ceramics graduate teaching and research program in the Metallurgy Department at what was then Case Institute of Technology, now a part of Case Western Reserve University. He continued to build the ceramics program, in particular by hiring some gifted faculty members and established what is generally recognized as one of the strongest programs of its kind. Al was made professor of ceramics at Case in 1968 and held that position until being named emeritus professor in 1992; by that time 40 percent of the Materials Science and Engineering Department's research was devoted to ceramics.

Alfred Cooper's major contributions lie in three areas: he identified and quantified chemical and physical factors that govern the continuous glass melting process; he clarified the conditions necessary for the formation of glass and the relationship of the resulting structures to glass properties; and he was prominent as an educator of glass technologists and ceramic engineers.

Al's work on glass melting enabled furnace designers and operators to increase the quality and quantity of glass fused in industrial furnaces. It is particularly effective in practical application, as it stems from his personal experiences during the early years he spent in glass manufacturing. His papers on mixing and melting of raw materials, heat transfer, and the flow of glass in furnaces are especially useful. Also valuable are his analyses of diffusion in glass and its effect on homogenization and refining of glass. His studies of the strength of glass fibers, particularly his classic work on field-assisted ion exchange, led to improvements in glass fiber strength.

In addition to clarifying the principles underlying glass manufacturing, Al made many contributions to a better understanding of glass structure. He was greatly interested in the random network theory of glass structure, and he eventually took a new approach, based network topology, that provided a general basis for a theory that fits most glassy systems and helps to account for their properties.

Those wishing to learn more about Cooper's work are referred to the excellent Festschrift prepared by P.K. Gupta and A.H. Heuer on the occasion of his retirement. It may be found in the *Journal of the American Ceramic Society*, Volume 76 (1993) pp. 1077-1080.

He had a deep conviction that international collaborations were important to the better understanding of glass phenomena and spent a substantial amount of time teaching and conducting research abroad. Al was a visiting professor at the University of Sheffield (1964 to 1965), at the Technical University of Clausthal, Germany, (1972 to 1973), the University of Padua, (1983), visiting lecturer at the Building Materials Research Institute, Beijing, (1983), and visiting professor at the Indian Institute of Technology, Kharagpur, (1986). He returned to India in 1988 as U.S. cochairman of the Indo-U.S. Workshop on Science and Technology of Glass at Bangalore. His international contributions were recognized by his election as fellow of the Society of Glass Technology (England), election to the Academy of Ceramics (Italy), and receiving the first President's Award of the International Commission on Glass (Beijing, 1995).

His teaching and research resulted in approximately 150 technical papers on glass and ceramics, as well as frequent participation in symposia and conferences. He twice chaired the Gordon Research Conferences: the 1968 Conference on Ceramics, and the 1972 Conference on Glass. He was also active in the American Ceramic Society (ACerS), serving as both chair and trustee of the Glass Division, and was recognized by his peers by election as a fellow, and finally, as a distinguished life member.

Al's contributions were also recognized by a number of awards, including the Raytheon Award of the New England Section of the ACerS, the George W. Morey Award of the Glass Division of the ACerS, the Toledo Glass and Ceramics Award of the Northwestern Ohio Section of the ACerS, the Eitel Award for excellence in silicate science from the University of Toledo, and the Samuel R. Scholes Award from Alfred University. He was also named the Edward Orton Distinguished Visiting Professor at Ohio State University in 1990. Cooper was elected to the National Academy of Engineering in 1996.

After he retired from Case Western Reserve in 1992, he continued to come in to his office regularly to write and discuss both scientific and social issues with students and faculty. Al enjoyed a wide variety of activities; among them were golf and tennis, gardening, jazz and classical music, dancing, and travel. When he traveled abroad, he liked particularly to go by sea, for the long, uninterrupted opportunity for thinking, or by train, for the opportunity to truly see the countryside. He also read and wrote poetry all his life (his favorite poets were Wallace Stevens and Baudelaire).

Al Cooper was an outstanding and beloved figure in glass technology, whose contributions were recognized throughout the world. Beyond his accomplishments, however, was this wise and gentle man; coupled with his finely honed intellectual curiosity was a passion for rigorous solutions to problems—a philosophy that he conveyed effectively to his students. Admired by his students and colleagues for his integrity, he was modest about his own achievements and preferred to talk to others about their accomplishments. His warm, sincere interest in others encouraged a generation of young people.

George A Deschamps

GEORGES A. DESCHAMPS

1911–1988

BY YUEN TZE LO, SHUNG-WU LEE, AND WENG CHO CHEW

OUR FRIEND GEORGES A. DESCHAMPS passed away on June 20, 1998, at the age of eighty-six after a long illness.

Deschamps was born in Vendome, France, on October 18, 1911, and studied mathematics at the École Normale Supérieure in Paris, one of the famous French "grandes écoles." Always fascinated by theoretical physics, he received advanced degrees in mathematics and physics from the Sorbonne, also in Paris. Then he served in the French Army as a lieutenant before coming to the United States in 1937 to spend a year at Princeton University. After that he taught mathematics and physics for about ten years at the Lycée Français de New York.

In 1947 Deschamps gave up teaching and became a project engineer with the Federal Telecommunication Laboratories, a division of International Telephone and Telegraph (ITT), where, among his many responsibilities, he worked on direction finding and radio navigation systems. It was at ITT that Deschamps invented a special-purpose quaternion computer for the solution of problems in inertial navigation. Geometric techniques always played a central role in his research. For example, he presented a unified description of a variety of transmission line, waveguide junction, and polarization problems in terms of a simple geometrical model. Based on this model, he developed graphical solution methods that he implemented in his "hyperbolic protractor." In many of his studies, Georges was a true forerunner. He developed a graphical representation of dispersion surfaces of wave propagation in magnetoplasmas and computed Fourier transforms by the fast Fourier transform method long before their "official appearance." He also suggested the early form of microstrip antennas before they become popular.

In 1958 Deschamps joined the University of Illinois at Urbana-Champaign as a professor of electrical engineering and director of the Antenna Laboratory. He discovered that a Gaussian beam can be represented by the radiation field from a point source located in a "complex" space. His discovery greatly simplifies many wave propagation problems of Gaussian beams. He worked the classical problem of diffraction by metal wedge, and developed a ray theory that is uniformly valid throughout transition regions near shadow boundaries.

From an engineering viewpoint, the biggest contribution Deschamps made is his formulation of the "divergence factor" of a ray pencil. The cross section of a ray pencil diverges or contracts as it is reflected from a material interface. Using his profound knowledge in geometry, Deschamps developed a matrix method for computing the divergence factor in an original and elegant manner. His method is being universally adopted in today's radar community for solving problems ranging from designing "stealth" airplanes to tracing signals from cellular telephones.

After his retirement in 1982, Deschamps spent many of his working hours on his favorite subject, differential forms. He predicted that in the future, Maxwell's equations would be taught by using differential forms instead of the present vector analysis. Judging by Deschamps record and his wisdom, his prediction may very well come true. Deschamps was a life fellow of the Institute of Electrical and Electronics Engineers (IEEE). He was elected to the National Academy of Engineering in 1978 with a citation that recognized his "contributions to electromagnetic scattering, microwave engineering, and laser beam propagation." In 1984 he received the IEEE Centennial Medal, and in 1987, the Antennas and Propagation Society Distinguished Achievement Award. He was an early participant and an active member of the International Scientific Radio Union.

Deschamps was a true scholar and an inspiring teacher. He was a man of great intellect, deeply insightful about electromagnetic theory, much sought after as a consultant by students and coworkers to whom he gave generously of his wisdom and expertise. Reserved, even shy, he was regarded with great affection by his many friends and colleagues. He indulged in his scientific endeavor and shared his knowledge, particularly his unique geometrical interpretation of electromagnetics, with colleagues even long after his retirement.

His wife, Bunty, his son, Francois, two daughters, Georgianne Gregg and Christiane, and five grandchildren survive him.

J. Presper Eckert

J. PRESPER ECKERT

1919–1995

BY LEO L. BERANEK

JOHN PRESPER ECKERT, or as he preferred, J. "Pres" Eckert, was born April 9, 1919, in Philadelphia, Pennsylvania. He received the bachelor of science degree from the University of Pennsylvania in 1941. His 1943 master of science degree in electrical engineering was from the University's Moore School of Electrical Engineering. Pres and his wife, Judith, had four children and made their home in Gladwyne, Pennsylvania. He was known as a serious worker who wanted things done right. His family and his students at the university attest to his readiness to be helpful and his devotion to vigorous and healthy living. He died June 3, 1995, in Bryn Mawr at the age of seventy-six.

A brilliant student, Pres was named a part-time laboratory instructor in his second graduate year at the Moore School. His charge was to teach the principles of engineering to students from other fields with the goal of making them able to work effectively in the World War II effort. His class comprised more than thirty students, sixteen of whom had their Ph.D.s. It was through that course that he met John W. Mauchly, whose doctorate was in physics.

In 1942 and 1943, Eckert became involved in improving a version of Vannevar Bush's differential analyzer, invented at the Massachusetts Institute of Technology. After considerable success, Mauchly and he discussed how much further its performance could be improved by more precisely machined parts and carefully controlled, air-conditioned space. They decided that this path was not fruitful. Together, they invented a digital differential analyzer, which was an electronic version of the mechanical Bush machine. Because it inefficiently counted pulses sequentially, they decided to build a machine that would use some sort of coded binary decimal system. This work proceeded slowly at first, because Eckert was doing graduate work and Mauchly was teaching. Mauchly then had the idea that an electrical device could be built that would have places to hold numbers, add numbers, and integrate equations. At that time, the only fast input and output equipment used punch cards, so the system had to be a combination of binary and coded decimal. But those ideas were sketchy.

Eckert contributed the engineering designs that made Mauchly's proposal practical. In early 1943, Mauchly wrote up their joint plans for this new type of computer. The Moore School knew that the army had critical needs for computing and that no existing machine was satisfactory. Using electromechanical calculators, the army was actively preparing ballistic tables to be used by the artillery crews in battle to determine the trajectories of missiles. The results were not very accurate. Thus, it was decided to seek funding for this proposed project from the U.S. Army Ballistics Research Laboratory in Aberdeen, Maryland. The presentation of the Eckert-Mauchly proposal was made by the department's administrator, John Brainard. Sometime before this date, Eckert had begun work on a mercury tank for measuring timing signals in connection with radar, arising from a request by MIT's Radiation Laboratory. Although this work had to be abandoned when the new project started, it would be important later.

The Eckert-Mauchly computer proposal was approved on April 9, 1943, and $150,000 was allocated for a machine with ten accumulators, a means for taking square roots using the Newton-Rapson method, and one function table with 104 entries, and so on. As time went on, the number of accumulators was doubled, a square root divider was substituted, and three function tables were mandated. The machine grew from eighteen panels to something like forty panels, and the appropriation was increased to about $400,000. Thus, the basis was in place for the development of the Electronic Numerical Integrator and Computer (ENIAC). Eckert was designated chief engineer on the project.

The ENIAC project called for vacuum tubes (transistors were not yet invented) and 18,000 were eventually used. Initial efforts were spent in learning how to extend their lives by reducing plate voltages and filament currents. Other memory ideas, such as recording magnetically on disks, were contemplated, but military urgency dictated that there could be no distraction from using vacuum tubes. There was external criticism about the mathematical basis for the calculations, which turned out later not to be important. On the hardware side, many questioned the feasibility of making 18,000 vacuum tubes work without failure for any significant length of time. Although statisticians predicted a mean free-path error of a couple of minutes, the results were greater by a hundred times or more than such predictions, or a lifetime of about 2,500 hours for each tube.

A staff of twelve professionals was involved in the development, and Eckert had to make the equipment decisions and the staff assignments, coordinate the activities, and finally develop means for testing the computer. Mauchly was more interested in programming, although he did some of the engineering, particularly in the final debugging of the completed machine. The computer was completed and ran its first real task in 1946. It measured about 2.5 meters in height and twenty-four meters in length. Programming was done by plug boards and switches. The computer, which was to operate until 1955, was more than 1,000 times faster than its electromechanical contemporaries and could execute up to 5,000 additions per second. An important feature was the subroutine scheme, which allowed the user to do an operation over and over until some criterion was met. This was handled through a special panel called a master programmer. Eckert explained, "The process of computing was carried on by 'accumulators.' Accumulators differ from a mechanical adding machine both because they are electronic and because you can control their start and finish, simultaneously transmit a number to one place as positive and to another as negative, and so forth."

Eckert next turned his attention to building a better machine. One vital improvement was the use of a mercury tank as the central memory, which was later supplanted by core memory. Incorporating it, a machine called the EDVAC was contemplated. Eckert and Mauchly left the Moore School in October 1946. Work on the EDVAC was continued by others at the Moore School.

Eckert and Mauchly founded the Electronic Control Company in October 1946. Their first order was received from Northrop Aircraft Company. That machine, called the Binary Automatic Computer (BINAC), was principally different in that it stored data on a magnetic tape rather than on punched cards.

The Electronic Control Company was renamed the Eckert-Mauchly Computer Corporation in 1949. They received an order from the National Bureau of Standards to build the Universal Automatic Computer (UNIVAC). Memory was the big problem—it finally evolved that a hierarchy of memories was necessary, as in today's computers. This was the first breakthrough. The second was the improvement of the subroutines, which led to internal programming. The UNIVAC, the first digital machine to be produced commercially in the United States, was delivered in 1951 to the United States Census Bureau. Eventually, forty-six UNIVACs were built. For the first time in computer history, a computing device was able to handle both numerical and alphabetical information with equal success. Mauchly, twelve years older than Eckert, left the company in 1950 and started his own consulting firm. He died in 1980.

In 1950 the Eckert-Mauchly Corporation was acquired by the Remington Rand Corporation and Eckert was appointed director of engineering of the Eckert-Mauchly Division. Successively, he was named vice-president and director of commercial engineering at Remington Rand (1955 to 1959), vice-president and executive assistant to the general manager of Remington-Rand (1959 to 1963), and vice-president and technical adviser to the president, Univac Division, Sperry Rand Corporation (1963 to 1982). When Sperry merged with the Burroughs Corporation to become Unisys in 1986, he stayed with the company and became a consultant. In 1989 Eckert retired from Unisys.

In 1968 the Honeywell Corporation challenged the patents covering the invention of the ENIAC computer. The presiding judge ruled in favor of Honeywell's claim that John Mauchly's ideas for electronic devices were obtained from meetings with John Vincent Atanasoff during a visit to Iowa in 1941. In an interview in 1981, Eckert stated that he and Mauchly had invented the computer "in the same sense that Edison invented the lightbulb." He said, "there were people who thought of the idea and tried to build one, but it didn't work very well."

In 1964 J. Presper Eckert received an honorary D.Sc. degree from the University of Pennsylvania. He was elected a member of the National Academy of Engineering in 1967. In January 1969 the National Medal of Science was awarded to Eckert by President Lyndon B. Johnson. In April 1969 he was awarded honorary membership in the Information Processing Society of Japan, and the "Eckert Award" was established in his honor for authors of best computer treatises. The Franklin Institute presented him with the Philadelphia Award in 1973.

Howard W. Emmons

HOWARD W. EMMONS

1912–1998

BY HOWARD R. BAUM AND GEORGE F. CARRIER

H OWARD WILSON EMMONS, the former Abbott and James Lawrence Professor of Engineering at Harvard University, died November 20, 1998, in Brigham and Women's Hospital, Boston, Massachusetts. He was active in the field of fire safety science, a subject shaped largely through his own efforts, until shortly before his death.

Professor Emmons was born August 30, 1912, in Morristown, New Jersey, the son of a carpenter. He attended local public schools and received a bachelor's degree in mechanical engineering from Stevens Institute of Technology in 1933, followed by an M.S. degree from the same institution in 1935. He spent the years 1935 to 1937 at Harvard University, obtaining a doctor of science degree in 1938. He was employed by the Westinghouse Electric and Manufacturing Company from 1937 to 1939 in the development of steam turbines. After one year as an associate professor at the University of Pennsylvania, he joined the faculty of Harvard University in 1940 and remained there until his retirement in 1983.

The accomplishments and contributions Professor Emmons made to engineering span a variety of fields. He was a leader in compressible flow research, discovering the basic propagating blade stall process responsible for the unsteady destructive performance of turbocompressors at low flow rates. He also discovered the existence of turbulent spots in the process of transition of fluid boundary layers from the laminar to the turbulent flow regime. His expertise in this field was by no means confined to laboratory experiments. He was one of the early contributors to the theory of compressible laminar boundary layers and served as the editor of *Fundamentals of Gas Dynamics*, volume III of the Princeton University Press series of books on high-speed aerodynamics and jet propulsion.

Professor Emmons also made novel contributions to many heat transfer problems. He introduced the use of numerical methods for solving partial differential equations to the heat transfer community as early as 1944, even before the development of the digital computer. He was a leader in studies of aerodynamic heating, and performed research in drying paper. His research in re-entry physics led to a combined laboratory and theoretical investigation of the thermodynamics and transport properties of plasmas at high pressures.

His expertise led to many committee assignments of national importance. These included membership on the Naval Technical Mission to Europe in 1945, commissioned to evaluate German technological advances in World War II, and membership on the Space Science and Technology Panel of the President's Scientific Advisory Council from 1958 to 1970. He was a founding member of the Committee on Fire Research in the National Research Council Division of Engineering, serving as a committee member from 1956 to 1972 and as chairman from 1967 to 1970. Professor Emmons's long connection with the National Bureau of Standards, now the National Institute of Standards and Technology (NIST), involved service on Panel 400, dealing with energy and heat transfer from 1967 to 1976. He chaired the Fire Panel 490 from 1971 to 1976 and the Evaluation Panel for the National Engineering Laboratory from 1980 to 1983.

Although his accomplishments were sufficient to warrant election to the National Academy of Engineering by 1965, and to the National Academy of Sciences a year later, the activities that dominated Professor Emmons's professional life from the mid-1960s until his death centered on fire safety research. His interest in fire phenomena began earlier, in the 1950s, due in part to the urging of Professor Hoyt Hottel of the Massachusetts Institute of Technology. An early result of this interest was his classic paper on what is now known in the combustion science community as the "Emmons Problem," *The Film Combustion of Liquid Fuel,* published in 1956. His growing involvement with fire safety issues led to his chairing the 1961 summer study on Fire Research at Woods Hole, Massachusetts, sponsored by the National Research Council. This study recommended the establishment of a federally funded program in fire research as the only realistic way to develop a scientific framework for fire protection engineering. It was a major step in a long process that led to passage of the Fire Research and Safety Act of 1968, for which he received an invitation to the White House. This in turn ultimately led to the establishment of coordinated fire research programs at the National Science Foundation and then at NIST.

While playing a leading role in the creation of fire research institutions in the United States, Professor Emmons's own research activities continued unabated. He devised a spectacular "fire whirl" experiment, demonstrating quantitatively how a cup-sized pool of liquid fuel can produce a flame several meters high (requiring a high-bay laboratory for its containment) under the combined influence of buoyancy and rotation. This was followed by a worldwide survey of fire safety measurements that demonstrated a nearly random variation in the ranking of materials from one country to the next. The "Home Fire Project," funded by the newly established Research Applied to National Needs Program at the National Science Foundation, was a collaboration between Harvard and the Basic Research Program (which he also helped found) at Factory Mutual Research Corporation. This project, started in 1972, continued until 1982, the year before Professor Emmons's retirement. The fifty-two technical reports (not counting archival publications) prepared under its auspices document the systematic development of the first predictive models of fire development in enclosures. The reports not only cover the development of the Harvard Computer Fire Code, which is the prototype for all subsequent work in this field, but also describe a wide range of careful experiments and theoretical analyses designed to provide a rigorous scientific underpinning to the computer model. This research continues on a worldwide basis to the present day. Bilateral collaborations with Japanese researchers in particular have benefited from Professor Emmons's involvement as a member of the U.S.-Japan Natural Resources Panel on Fire Research and Safety. He was a lively participant at the fourteenth meeting of the panel in June 1998 in Tokyo.

Professor Emmons was the recipient of many honors in addition to those cited above. He was awarded the Edgerton Gold Medal in 1968 by the Combustion Institute, the Timoshenko Medal in 1971 by the American Society of Mechanical Engineers, three awards including an honorary doctor of science degree in 1963 from the Stevens Institute of Technology, and an honorary doctor of science degree from Worcester Polytechnic Institute in 1983. He also won the Man of the Year Award from the Society of Fire Protection Engineers and the Fluid Dynamics Prize from the American Physical Society in 1982.

Although he never had more than a handful of graduate students at any one time, Professor Emmons guided fifty-one doctoral candidates to their Ph.D.s. Many of these students, in turn, became faculty members at major research universities or leaders in government and industrial research organizations. His influence on colleagues both at Harvard and elsewhere was no less significant. His ability to get to the root of a technical issue and clarify the thinking of almost anyone he interacted with was uncanny. Perhaps equally important was his ability to accomplish this without unduly bruising the egos of those engaged in these conversations. It is hard to forget the technical intensity of many of the lunchtime discussions among members of the applied mechanics group at Harvard, which more than one junior faculty member regarded as being more demanding than their oral Ph.D. qualifying exam.

A more relaxed atmosphere could be found at Professor Emmons's home in Sudbury, Massachusetts. He and his wife, Dorothy, were married in 1938. They moved onto an old farm in the then-rural town in the early 1940s, shortly after he joined the Harvard faculty. They raised their daughter, Beverly, and sons, Scott and Keith there, on a property that included a barn, apple orchards, and a vegetable garden. The Emmons family enjoyed hosting picnics for colleagues, neighbors, and students. An added attraction in later years was the swimming pool and tennis court they built on their land. In addition to improving his home, Professor Emmons took considerable interest in the Sudbury public schools, which the children attended, as well as the local town government. Sudbury was (and indeed still is) governed by the traditional New England open town meeting, providing yet another outlet for his abilities. He was a member of the Lincoln-Sudbury School Committee for seventeen years starting in 1946 and a Selectman for the Town of Sudbury from 1969 to 1972. He and Dorothy remained together in Sudbury until her death in 1990. Two of their children, Beverly and Scott, currently live in Brooklyn, New York. Their youngest son, Keith, is a resident of Los Gatos, California. There are three grandchildren.

EUGENE G. FUBINI

1913–1997

BY BOB O. EVANS

In MY FIFTY-ONE YEARS OF PROFESSIONAL LIFE, from the vantage point of being an IBM general management executive, a venture capitalist, an executive in a high technology consulting firm, president of a Taiwan semiconductor company, president of an advanced electronics company and chairman of a leading software technology company, I have met some of the world's greatest scientists, engineers, government and corporate executives, heads of state, educators and working people. Of all those met in my lengthy business life, the most remarkable is Dr. Eugene Fubini.

This brilliant and amazing man, perhaps five feet tall in his shoes, was a bundle of vibrant energy with infinite curiosity, compassion, warmth, and knowledge far beyond his training as a physicist. He had an abiding love for his adopted country and made significant contributions to hundreds of projects from his early days as a young engineer at Columbia Broadcasting System. He began to hit his stride as a research associate during World Was II at the famed Harvard Radio Research Laboratory, where he led advances in electronic countermeasures and reconnaissance equipment.

After the war, Dr. Fubini spent sixteen productive years at the Airborne Instruments Laboratory Company, where he continued to innovate in the field of reconnaissance electronics. He produced numerous patents in electromagnetics and microwave applications.

In March 1961 his opportunity for contributions enlarged significantly as he joined the Department of Defense (DOD) as director of research in the Office of Director, Defense Research and Engineering. He had great influence on DOD research and engineering, and his reputation rapidly became international. In two short years he was promoted to assistant secretary of defense for research and engineering and was a key part of a famed team of DOD executives.

In 1965 I became president of IBM's Federal Systems Division and longed to have access to such an important leader. However, Dr. Fubini tended to DOD business and tried to avoid sales calls by all-too-anxious defense contractors. In 1966 Dr. Fubini joined IBM as a vice-president responsible for research and other advanced development operations. Because the Federal Systems Division's activities were close to Dr. Fubini's heart, I had the great fortune of becoming a close and admiring friend. Because of his reputation for brilliance, Dr. Fubini was in great demand by the aerospace community and, occasionally, agreed to review a project. I recall vividly one instance where a major corporation had invested two years of effort on an advanced system and they anxiously wanted Fubini's overview. Dr. Fubini agreed to review the project and invited me to observe. After the company's well-prepared presentation, Dr. Fubini not only showed them why their concept was fatally flawed, but he did it in such a way that they accepted his critique and the project was terminated, probably saving the company millions of dollars and, possibly the federal government hundreds of millions of dollars!

Many a night have I spent at the Fubini's home or he at mine. The invigorating discussions still influence me. I watched as his adoring wife, Betty, brought tea and cookies to our late-night discussions. I have watched him tell each of his six loving children good night and seen the warmth in his eyes for all of his family.

Sadly for IBM, Dr. Fubini left after two years and returned to his first love, the business of the DOD. He became a consultant and was in high demand. From my direct knowledge, Dr. Fubini contributed again and again in guiding not only companies but also the DOD in his role as chairman of the Defense Science Board.

Gene Fubini was remarkable as he positively influenced all the people who were in contact with him and steered technologies to high purpose. His brilliance wisely guided the Defense Department as well as many aerospace companies. The world lost a great professional when Gene Fubini passed away—yet his legacy continues.

DONALD F. GALLOWAY

1913–1996

BY M. EUGENE MERCHANT

DONALD F. GALLOWAY, founder and retired director general of the Production Engineering Research Association of Great Britain, died on December 21, 1996, at the age of eighty-three. Don was born on March 22, 1913, in Birmingham, England. He received a thorough grounding in fundamental knowledge from his British secondary school education. Following this, Don first served an engineering apprenticeship with Birmingham Small Arms Machine Tools and then attended Birmingham Technical College. Upon graduation, he entered Cambridge University, but his studies there were interrupted as he took up an invitation to go briefly to Canada. When he returned, he resumed his pursuit of a university education in earnest, and earned a London External B.Sc. degree in engineering in 1936.

During his engineering studies, he developed a strong interest in manufacturing and decided to begin his career by employment in that industry. He therefore accepted an offer of employment at Birmingham Small Arms Machine Tool Company in the position of designer of machine tools. In 1937 he joined Dunlop Rubber Company, Birmingham, as a designer for plant automation. However, he soon began to realize that his real interest was to become involved in engineering research in the field of manufacturing. In 1939 he had the good fortune to secure a position as assistant director at the Institution of Production Engineers, the technical society serving engineers employed in the British manufacturing industry. This gave him the opportunity to simultaneously pursue graduate study, culminating in his being awarded a Ph.D., external, by London University in 1943. In 1944 he was made director of research at the Institution of Production Engineers.

By this time, Don's interest in manufacturing research had sharpened still further, and he became particularly inquisitive about its effects on the manufacturing industry as whole. He therefore began to travel extensively on the European continent, as well as in Britain, to observe and discuss the research being done in this field in both industry and academia. This produced two outcomes that had salutary effects, not only on his career, but also on that of other manufacturing engineers worldwide. First, he had come to realize that world manufacturing industry of that time was in serious need of a highly competent source of industry-oriented manufacturing research and development, to increase its productivity and effectiveness. Second, through his travels he had become well acquainted with the leading people in manufacturing research in Britain and on the continent at that time, most of whom were engaged in such research in universities.

Regarding the first of these outcomes, Don, in his position as director of research at the Institution of Production Engineers, had already become extremely successful in planning and organizing industrial research and in promoting cooperation among engineering organizations and specialists in the field of manufacturing. As a result, he became convinced that industrial firms could benefit greatly from cooperative research on their common manufacturing problems. As a consequence of this conviction, together with his previously mentioned recognition of the serious need for a highly competent source of industry-oriented manufacturing research and development, in 1946 Don took the bold move of organizing and founding the now world-renowned Production Engineering Research Association (PERA) of Great Britain, headquartered in Melton Mowray, United Kingdom. He served as the director general of PERA until 1978, when he retired. Under his dynamic leadership, these famous PERA laboratories came to serve the needs of thousands of factories spread among many countries throughout the world.

Don was always determined that the results of PERA's research be properly applied in industry. As part of this philosophy, he persuaded the British government to take the unusual action of supporting various in-plant projects. For example, this included such programs as the PERA Mobile Demonstration Unit, which visited companies to introduce and demonstrate the new technologies and techniques that PERA's research and development had developed. This program evolved into the Production Engineering Advisory Service, which provided advice and assistance covering the whole spectrum of manufacturing activities. Over the years, the PERA laboratories carried out extensive and highly productive cooperative manufacturing research and development for a great variety of manufacturing companies, to solve their manufacturing problems. In many cases, this yielded immense improvements in their productivity, profitability, and competitiveness. Eventually, PERA grew to become one of Europe's leading multiskilled organizations specializing in management consulting, technology, business research, and training. Its staff of 400 operated from four sites in the United Kingdom and one office in Spain, assisting its worldwide client base with the development of competitive manufacturing and business strategies.

As for the second of the two outcomes referred to above, that of Don's wide acquaintance with the leading people engaged in manufacturing research in Britain and on the continent, this also culminated in a highly beneficial event for manufacturing research. That event evolved from a close relationship that he developed in the late 1940s with three distinguished manufacturing researchers in three other countries. These were Professor E. Bickel of the Technical University of Zurich (Switzerland), Professor O. Peters of the Catholic University of Leuven (Belgium), and General P. Nicolau, director of the research arm of the French military (France). These three shared Don's conviction that the development of new manufacturing technology was being hampered by the lack of appropriate manufacturing research. Further, they also all felt strongly that there was an urgent need for joint action in this area. They also realized that, in view of the importance and scale of the problems to be tackled, only international cooperative action among manufacturing researchers would be effective. Discussions among the four resulted in their conception and establishment of a mechanism to accomplish just this. This was the foundation, in 1951, of the International Institution for Production Research (CIRP). Membership in this society was limited to leading manufacturing researchers from the various industrialized countries of the world, selected by vote of the members. This membership pattern was intended to ensure maximum efficiency in international communication, cooperation, and participation among the members, and has done so very effectively. The collective influence of that society, which now has members in thirty-eight countries, has had a unique and salutary impact on improvements in manufacturing operations, worldwide. Don was extremely active in it from the start and served as its president from 1959 to 1960.

Don was not only a capable executive and organizer, but also a capable researcher in his own right. He won early recognition for his landmark research on the drilling process, one of the most widely used and critical processes employed by the manufacturing industry worldwide. He also conducted very important original research on the effects of machine tool design, maintenance practices, and human factors on productivity of manufacturing operations. But he made important contributions to industrial productivity in many other ways as well and also received many awards and other recognition for his outstandingly effective efforts, in many fields, to advance the capabilities of the world manufacturing industry. Among his most significant publications are the following:

- *Practical Drilling Tests* (book) with I. S. Morton, Institution of Production Engineers, 1947.
- "Production Engineering Research and Its Practical Applications in Britain." American Society of Mechanical Engineers, 1956 (Calvin W. Rice Lecture).
- "Machine Tool Research, Design and Utilization," Institution of Mechanical Engineers, 1960 (James Clayton Lecture).

- "Production Engineering Research and the Common Market," *The Production Engineer*, 1951.
- "Technology, Economy and Philosophy of Improving Productivity in Manufacturing Industries," Institute of Production Engineers, 1968.
- "Mankind and Manufacture." Presidential Address to the Institution of Production Engineers, 1969.
- "Technology Transfer for Manufacturing Industries." AGARD Conference, Paris, 1978.

He was elected to the council of the Institution of Mechanical Engineers in 1950 and elected as its president in 1969. He was also a fellow of that institution and of the Institution of Production Engineers. In 1973 he helped organize the Engineers Registration Board, representing fifty-two English institutions, and was its chairman through 1979. He also served on the Council of Engineering Institutions from 1973 to 1978. He was awarded a CBE (Commander of the British Empire) by Queen Elizabeth II in 1962 in recognition of his service to the nation. In 1978 he was made an honorary member of the Society of Manufacturing Engineers (USA). In that same year, Don received the high honor of being chosen for membership in the newly formed Fellowship of Engineering (now the Royal Academy of Engineering), the British equivalent of the U.S. National Academy of Engineering and served as leader of its Group A (marine, mechanical, aeronautical, production engineering) during 1978 to 1979. After his retirement from PERA in 1978, he served as a private consultant, mostly at the governmental level, for seven countries in the Far East. He also was a leader in developing a national plan for improving productivity in the United Kingdom, based on his earlier work. He was elected to membership in the National Academy of Engineering, as a foreign associate, in 1984.

Don had an engaging personality and, in addition, a marvelous British-style sense of humor, making him very popular, not only with his male peers but also with their ladies. Don's strong passion for manufacturing research, while being his most consuming one, was by no means his only one. He pursued a variety of others with great vigor throughout his full life. In his youth,

Don was a keen athlete and won several mile and half-mile events in the British Midlands Championships. He also enjoyed playing tennis. Later in life he became interested in farming and particularly in the breeding of pedigreed Galloway cattle, a hobby that persisted throughout most of the rest of his life. He also had a penchant for fine horses. He acquired a farm, named Roecliffe in Charnwood, located near Loughborough in Leicestershire, England, made it home for himself and his lovely wife, Toni, and stocked it with the finest of pedigreed Belted Galloways and some elegant riding horses. We remember with pleasure our many visits there, a part of each of which was always to be taken on a tour of its meadows, spiced with Don's humor, to admire and enjoy the cattle and horses. Further, when he came to visit us in Ohio, a must of the visit was a tour into Kentucky to see the Man 'o War's statue and grave, visit the horse farms (where he had the most famous of the horses paraded out for him), and visit farms that bred Belted Galloway cattle.

Another of Don's passions was CIRP, of which he was a co-founder. He lavished his time and effort on it to ensure its success. And when its annual General Assembly finally met for the first time in Britain, in 1958, he left no stone unturned to make it the most outstanding such meeting in that society's history up to then. He unleashed the entire staff of PERA's Conference Division on it, ensuring impeccable operation of both the technical sessions and programs and the social events, including the social programs for the ladies. To quote from the "Ladies Programs" portion of the written history of CIRP, "Justice was most assuredly done to 'England's Green and Pleasant Land'—to the ancient capitol of the British people sitting on the banks of the river Thames—to its abbeys, cathedrals, castles, stately homes, its universities, market towns and its storybook villages. Dr. and Mrs. Galloway were absolutely convinced that visitors to England could not have a good time, or understand what they were seeing or doing, without a few pointers; and a few pointers they were given—to put it modestly." In 1968 the CIRP General Assembly was again held in Britain and once more Don and PERA hosted it. To again quote the CIRP history, "It would be safe to say that THE HIGHLIGHT of the meeting was the afternoon the men and women spent at the farm of Dr. and Mrs. Galloway at Roecliffe in Charnwood. We wandered through the gray stone house which rose above terraced gardens. We admired the farm buildings and even strolled a distance to observe the magnificent herd of cattle grazing in the meadows—Belted Galloways, of course."

Don and his wife, Toni, had one daughter, Toni Ann, who often attended the CIRP General Assemblies with them until she married. She and her husband, Anthony Charter, then moved to Hong Kong, where, until his recent retirement, he held the position of manager of the notorious old Kai Tak Hong Kong International Airport. Don's wife, Toni, unfortunately died in 1984. He later remarried and, with his new wife, Mary, he created a new home and a lovely garden at Morcott in Rutland, England.

Don was a consummate engineer, an inspired and inspiring leader, and truly a gentleman and a scholar in every sense of those words! He is deeply missed, indeed, by all who knew him well.

H. Joseph Gerber

H. JOSEPH GERBER

1924–1996

BY ANTHONY J. DeMARIA

H. JOSEPH GERBER, founder, board chairman, former chief executive officer, and president of Gerber Scientific, Inc. of South Windsor, Connecticut, died August 8, 1996, at a hospital in Hartford, Connecticut. He was seventy-two years old.

Joe was born on April 7, 1924, in Vienna, Austria. He became a U.S. citizen in 1945. He was imprisoned in a Nazi labor camp at age fifteen, and came to the United States from Vienna about 1940. He arrived with few possessions and without a strong command of English. He graduated from Rensselaer Polytechnic Institute in Troy, New York, with a B.S. degree in aeronautical engineering in 1946. He started inventing new measurement and calculation tools while in college. In 1948 Joe founded Gerber Scientific with about $3,000. The company, based in South Windsor, Connecticut, now employees about 28,000 people and had revenues of just under $600 million in fiscal year 1999. He is survived by his wife, whom he married in 1953, a son, who is a director and a vice-president of business development and technology strategy at Gerber Scientific, and a daughter. Mr. Gerber is a classic rags-to-tech-riches story. He had over 648 U.S. and foreign patents issued in his name.

As a junior at Rensselaer, he invented a graphical numerical computer called the Gerber Variable Scale. At the time, it was called the most revolutionary engineering tool since the slide rule. It was the first product to launch the Gerber Scientific

Instrument Company. For nearly five decades, Joe Gerber was
the driving force behind Gerber Scientific's evolution from a
one-product company to a major supplier of intelligent manufacturing systems. Today, Gerber Scientific, Inc. comprises the
following wholly owned subsidiaries:

- Gerber Coburn, the world leader in ophthalmic lens
  processing systems.
- Gerber Scientific Products, the world leader in the
  development and manufacture of computerized sign
  making and specialty graphics systems, software, materials,
  and accessories.
- Spandex, the leading global distributor of high-
  performance software and equipment for the sign making
  and specialty graphics industry.
- Gerber Technology, the world leader in advanced
  computer-aided design and manufacturing systems for
  producing industrial, commercial, and retail sewn goods.
- Gerber Innovations, the world leader in steel rule die
  production systems for the packaging industry.

On September 14, 1994, H. Joseph Gerber was awarded our
nation's highest honor for technological achievement, the National Medal of Technology, for his contributions toward advancing manufacturing technology through his many inventions and
for his significant contributions to our nation's economic competitiveness. The citation for Mr. Gerber's award reads: "For his
past and continuing technical leadership in the invention, development and commercialization of manufacturing automation
systems for a wide variety of industries—most notably apparel—
that have made those industries more efficient and cost-effec-
tive in today's worldwide competitive environment." The award
was bestowed by Vice President Al Gore.

In nominating Mr. Gerber for the award, Roland W. Schmitt,
president emeritus of Rensselaer Polytechnic Institute, said, "It
is my belief that this dynamic individual embodies the very essence of what the award represents; he is a prolific inventor, a
successful entrepreneur, and a highly accomplished engineer."

On June 8, 1995, Joe Gerber was awarded Connecticut's first

Annual Connecticut Medal of Technology. Professor D. Allan Bromley of Yale University, chairman of the selection committee, stated that Mr. Gerber was presented Connecticut's First Medal of Technology Award for "His extraordinary achievements in commercialization of technology in one or more of the areas of process and product innovation management that has made a significant difference in Connecticut's industrial competitiveness."

For nearly a quarter of a century, Mr. Gerber made exceptional technological contributions that rank among the milestones in the history of the textile industry. The innovation for which Joe Gerber is best known is the GERBERcutter®, which automatically cuts large quantities of material with a computer controlled knife and is considered to be the industries single most important advancement in this century. The American Apparel Manufacturer's Association has stated that the GERBERcutter® was a significant weapon in the apparel industry's ongoing fight for market share against low-wage imports. Furthermore, his inventions played a major role in allowing the apparel industry to maintain a large and diverse domestic production base, providing jobs for thousands of Americans.

In addition to the invention of the Variable Scale graphical computer in the 1940s, he also invented the Derivemeter, which gives the derivative of a graph or curve, the Equameter, which gives the equation of a curve, and the Graph Analogue, an improved version of the variable scale in the 1950s.

The first production unit of the GERBERcutter® is now in the possession of the Smithsonian's National Museum of American History in Washington, D.C. The unit was originally sold to General Motors Fisher Body Division in 1970 and for more than twenty-two years was in continuous operation cutting car seat covers and other soft goods for automobile interiors. Three of Mr. Gerber's original scientific instruments are also in the permanent collection of the National Museum of American History. All three artifacts—the Variable Scale, Graph Analogue, and Derivemeter—were on display in the museum exhibition titled "Information Age: People, Information, and Society" in 1994.

In recognition of his technical contributions, Joe Gerber was awarded an honorary doctor of engineering degree by the Rensselaer Polytechnic Institute in 1981 and by the University of New Haven in 1990. He was elected to the National Academy of Engineering in 1982. His citation read: "By combining pragmatism with imagination, and hard work with optimism, he has become one of American's most prolific and successful inventors." He was elected to membership of the Connecticut Academy of Science and Engineering in 1983. He was a recipient of the Connecticut Patent Law Association's Tenth Annual Eli Whitney Award in 1980, the Holden Medal for his outstanding contribution to the advancement of technology in the apparel industry in 1983, the ORT Science and Technology Award in 1988, the Lifetime Achievement Award in Entrepreneurial Management in 1989, and the Companion Membership Award of the Textile Institute in 1993.

Dr. Gerber served on the board of directors of the following organizations: Boston Digital Corporation in Milford, Massachusetts; Beta Engineering and Development Ltd., Been Sheva, Israel; and the Phoenix Mutual Insurance Company in Hartford, Connecticut. He was a trustee for the Hartford Graduate Center in Hartford, and an honoree trustee of the Rensselaer Polytechnic Institute in Troy, New York.

E. L. Ginzton

EDWARD L. GINZTON

1915–1998

BY EDWARD J. BARLOW

Edward Leonard Ginzton, retired chief executive officer of Varian Associates, died on August 13, 1998. He was born on December 27, 1915, in Dnepropetrovsk, Ukraine. He was the son of Leonard Louis and Natalia P. (Philipova) Ginzton. Ed came to the United States in 1929 and attended public school in San Francisco. He received his B.S. in electrical engineering from the University of California in 1936 and an M.S. in 1937; he received his E.E. degree in 1938 and his Ph.D. in 1940 from Stanford University. He married Artemas A. McCann on June 6, 1939, and they had four children: Anne, Leonard, Nancy, and David.

Ed was a research engineer at Sperry Gyroscope Company on Long Island from 1940 to 1946. He was assistant professor of applied physics from 1946 to 1947, associate professor of applied physics from 1947 to 1950, and professor of applied physics from 1951 to 1968, all at Stanford. He was also the director of the Microwave Laboratory at Stanford from 1949 to 1959 and the director of the Stanford University Project M (the SLAC linear accelerator) from 1957 to 1960.

Ed was instrumental in the founding of Varian Associates. He was a director of Varian from 1948 until 1993. He was chairman of the board from 1959 to 1984 and chief executive officer from 1959 to 1972. From 1964 to 1968, he was also president. He was chairman of the executive committee of the board from 1984 to 1993.

While at Sperry during World War II, Ed was instrumental in furthering the development of klystron tubes, pulse-Doppler radar, and microwave measurements. He had a vision that klystron tubes could be scaled up in power by a factor of 1,000 successfully. Later at Stanford, he continued his work to stimulate development of ever higher power klystrons such as those that power SLAC today. Klystron and other microwave tubes were further encouraged at Varian. The pulse-Doppler techniques initially developed under Ed's direction at Sperry are the predominant features of many sophisticated radars today.

At Stanford's Microwave Laboratory, with Ed's participation and under his direction, linear accelerator concepts and devices were developed and improved. This led to the construction of linear accelerators for particle physics research. The early accelerators—the Mark I, Mark II, and Mark IV—were a few 10s to 100s of feet long. Ed was instrumental in the early stages of Project M, the SLAC accelerator project, an accelerator two miles long, both in stimulating the engineering work required and in getting federal funding. Here again, an enormous scale-up was found to be feasible. The Mark IV accelerator was built to test the concepts for the SLAC design.

Another application of the linear accelerator concept was for the treatment of cancer. The Mark IV was used for early experiments in this application. Ed was a crusader for the use of the accelerator in cancer treatment and although this use took many years to come to fruition, there are some 4,000 machines in use in the world today treating more than one million patients annually. Under Ed's leadership, Varian acquired the predominant market share for this equipment.

Another idea germinated in the early years at Stanford and at Sperry was that of nuclear magnetic resonance, or NMR. Ed supported the continuing development of NMR machines at Varian for many years, and Varian is today the leading manufacturer of such instruments worldwide. Ed also had a vision of building a company with a group of analytical instruments, so over the years mass spectrometers, atomic absorption instruments, gas and liquid chromatographs, and UV-visible spectrophotometers were added to NMR to make the instrument company of today.

Ed was elected to the National Academy of Engineering in 1965 (and was a member of its Council from 1974 to 1980) and to the National Academy of Sciences in 1966. He was involved in many committees of the Academies, including the National Research Council Division of Engineering Committee on Motor Vehicle Emissions (chair, 1971 to 1972), the Assembly of Engineering Committee on Nuclear and Alternative Energy Systems (cochair), the National Academy of Sciences' Panel on Scientific Communications and National Security, and the joint Institute of Medicine/Commission on Life Sciences Committee on the Use of Animals in Biomedical and Behavioral Research. He was also a member of the National Academy of Sciences Delegation to Hungary (1966), Bulgaria (1972), and the USSR (1973 and 1975). He was a member of the Academy Commission on International Relations, 1977 to 1980.

Ed received many honors. He was a fellow of the Institute of Electrical and Electronics Engineers and was on its board of directors and chairman of its Awards Board. He received the Morris Liebmann Memorial Prize and the Medal of Honor. He received the California Manufacturer of the Year Award in 1977 and was inducted into the Silicon Valley Engineering Hall of Fame in 1995. He was a member of Sigma Xi, Eta Kappa Nu, and Tau Beta Pi.

Ed also served on boards and committees beyond his immediate Varian and Stanford connections. To name a few, he served as a director of the Stanford Bank, chairman of the Advisory Board of the School of Engineering at Stanford, a member of the Stanford University board of trustees, board of directors of Stanford University Hospital, Lawrence Berkeley Laboratory Scientific and Educational Advisory Committee, and board of directors of the National Bureau of Economic Research.

Much of Ed's work at the Microwave Laboratory at Stanford concerned microwave measurement techniques. With this background, he wrote the book *Microwave Measurements* as part of the *International Series of Pure and Applied Physics*, published in 1957. Ed also contributed articles to technical journals. He was the sole inventor for twenty-two patents and the joint inventor for another seventeen, mostly in the fields of microwave measurements and components.

Ed had wide-ranging interests beyond his professional life. He loved to restore old cars and had a model A Ford, which looked brand new. He was an avid and talented photographer and made many striking pictures, particularly of outdoor scenes—mountains, meadows, flowers, and rivers.

He loved to travel. With various members of his family, he traveled over Africa in a hot air balloon. He attended a banquet in the Saudi Arabian desert, visited Machu Picchu, saw the great pyramids and the Sphinx, visited the Great Wall of China, went through the Grand Canyon, and went around the world stopping in New Zealand and Hawaii.

Ed had strong interests in bettering the community. He championed the causes of fair housing and clean air. With David Packard and later Pief Panofsky, he co-chaired the Stanford Mid-Peninsula Urban Coalition, which helped launch minority-owned small businesses. He worked on related education and health issues and on the need for affordable housing, serving as a member of the board of directors of the Mid-Peninsula Housing Development Corporation.

Ed had a collegial management style. He encouraged us all to work wholeheartedly and independently on what we thought was most important. His concept is expressed in the word "Associates" in the name Varian Associates. Many of the developments mentioned above such as the high-power klystrons, pulse-Doppler radar, linear accelerators for medical research, SLAC, and NMR grew out of intense collaboration with associates such as Bill Hansen, Russell and Sigurd Varian, Marvin Chodorow, Pief Panofsky, John Woodyard, and Myrl Stearns, among others. Ed was truly a man of broad interests and large and persistent vision, who enjoyed life to the fullest and cared about his family, his associates, and his community.

ANDRÉ Y. GIRAUD

1925–1997

BY CHAUNCEY STARR

O N JULY 27, 1997, one of the French nuclear energy community's most prominent figures, André Giraud, died. A former administrator general of the French Atomic Energy Commission from 1970 to 1978, minister of industry from 1978 to 1981, and minister of defense from 1986 to 1988, André Giraud was involved in all major decisions that resulted in the French national nuclear electricity program. André Giraud was a friend to the United States. During his career he developed a privileged relationship with all major nuclear scientists and representatives and in 1977 became a foreign associate of the U.S. National Academy of Engineering. In 1980 Giraud received the prestigious American Nuclear Society/Nuclear Energy Institute Henry DeWolf Smyth Award.

André Giraud was born in Bordeaux, France, on April 3, 1925. He was a graduate of École Polytechnique (Paris), École Nationale Supérieure des Mines (Paris), and École Nationale Supérieure du Pétrole. From 1949 to 1950, André trained in the United States, focusing on the petrochemical industry. He then resumed his career in France, working as a researcher, then executive vice-president, of the French Institute of Petroleum from 1951 to 1964.

Between the years of 1964 and 1990, André was either in charge of, a member of, or worked with many important institutions and companies such as the French Oil Directorate (head), minister of education (chief aide), Atomic Energy Commissariat (chairman), Energy and Industry in the Barre government (secretary), Paris-Dauphine University (professor), the Chirac government (secretary for defense), and the Compagnie Générale d'Innovation et de Dévelopment (president).

Other achievements attained by André Giraud between the years of 1974 and 1994 include being chairman of the French Scientific Council of Defense, chairman of the International Advisory Board of the Elf Group, and president of Ecole Polytechnique.

Along with the Henry de Wolfe-Smythe Award, André also received the Foratom Award given by the European Nuclear Society, the Honorary Medal of the French Nuclear Society, and various French and foreign decorations, including Commandeur de la Légion d'Honneur.

This long and wide-ranging career in service to France was indicative of André Giraud's capabilities as an administrator and an imaginative leader. In international relations he was recognized as a politician of exceptional vision and dimension. He emphasized long-term perspectives, while alertly considering near-term steps. He was an intuitive and knowledgeable diplomat who established warm personal relationships with members of foreign governments. This was particularly important to France in the key area of energy supplies during a time when oil and gas imports faced much international turbulence.

André Giraud was actively involved in keeping France in the forefront of international science and technology. His outstanding intellect, exceptional capacity for synthesis, and openness to imaginative innovation made him a persuasive leader of the French technology scene. He was an active promoter of new concepts and was able to put them into practice by his great ability to organize and manage the implementing institutions. His footprints are evident throughout many French national programs, including programs in the space, military, and energy fields. He was deeply involved in the development of the French nuclear power system, making it one of the world's best, and he was committed to the goal that it become a long-term indigenous resource for the country. He courageously took the responsibility of abandoning the early French uranium-graphite reactors and adopting the U.S.-developed pressurized water reactors, and supported a fast breeder project to achieve uranium independence.

André Giraud was one of the most prestigious foreign associates of the National Academy of Engineering. As a consequence of his warm and friendly personality, and his consideration for all he worked with, he will remain in the memories of a long list of friends and associates.

John M Granger

JOHN V. N. GRANGER

1918–1997

BY JOHN R. WHINNERY

J OHN VAN NUYS GRANGER, antenna and telecommunications expert, entrepreneur, and public servant, died December 1, 1997, in Cirencester, England. He was born in Cedar Rapids, Iowa, on September 14, 1918. After attending the Cedar Rapids Academy of Art, he graduated from Cornell College, Mt. Vernon, Iowa, with a B.A. degree in mathematics and physics in 1941. He did graduate work at Harvard University, where he earned an M.S. degree in communications engineering in 1942 and a Ph.D. degree in applied physics in 1948. From 1942 to 1946, he was a civilian employee of Harvard University in the Radio Research Laboratory and the American-British Laboratory and was a technical observer for the NDRC Division 15 with the U.S. Forces in Europe from 1944 to 1945.

Following completion of his doctorate, John joined the Stanford Research Institute in Menlo Park, California. As assistant director of engineering, he directed the research programs for U.S. government sponsors and prime contractors. His own research was concentrated on aircraft antennas, especially slot antennas that could be mounted flush with the aircraft surface and thus minimize aerodynamic drag. He was author or coauthor of numerous technical reports and journal articles on design and measurement of antennas of this class and on their integration into telecommunication systems.

In 1956 he founded Granger Associates in Palo Alto, California, and served as president. Initial emphasis was on antennas, especially broadband antennas of the log periodic type, and two unique products, ionospheric sounders to optimize short wave transmissions, and null-field precipitation static dischargers to minimize the buildup of electrostatic charge on aircraft surfaces. These dischargers became standard equipment on all jet aircraft made in the United States. A wide range of communication equipment followed. Because there was broad international acceptance of the systems, two subsidiaries were formed, Granger Associates Ltd., Weybridge, England, and Granger Associates (Pty) Ltd., Sydney, Australia, with John as chairman. His concern was that all Granger Associate products be of high quality and that all employees feel a sense of pride in their contribution and in the company. Indeed there was a strong sense of family among Granger Associate employees.

John was active in his professional societies, serving as a director of the West Coast Electronics Show, WESCON, as an editorial reviewer for the Institute of Radio Engineers, and as editor of its *Transactions on Antennas and Propagation.* In the Institute of Electrical and Electronics Engineers (IEEE), he was a member of the awards board, chairman of the Finance Committee, and treasurer. He was a member of the IEEE board of directors and executive committee of IEEE and was elected its president in 1970. This was a time of rapid growth of the institute, and to give proper attention to the issues of this growth, John resigned his presidency of Granger Associates.

Following completion of his term as IEEE president, John spent the remainder of his career in government service with emphasis on policy concerning international issues of science and technology. With the Department of State, Washington, D.C., 1971 to 1975, he was acting director of the Bureau of International Scientific and Technological Affairs and deputy assistant secretary, Bureau of Oceans. With the National Science Foundation, 1975 to 1977, he was deputy director of the Office of Science and Technology Policy and deputy assistant director for scientific, technological and international affairs. He was Counselor for Scientific and Technological Affairs for the U.S. Embassy, London, and Science Attaché to the U.S. Embassy in Paris. The issues he saw in these assignments led to the well-received book *Technology and International Relations* (W. H. Freeman and Company, 1979).

On the basis of John's technical, management, and policy contributions, he was elected to the National Academy of Engineering in 1975. Among other recognitions he received were the Outstanding Young Electrical Engineer Award of Eta Kappa Nu in 1952, the IRE's Seventh Region Electronic Achievement Award in 1955, and fellow status in the IEEE.

Following retirement in 1983, he moved with wife, Jill (Norah Frances) to a 300-year-old stone cottage in the Cotswolds area of England, where he concentrated on nontechnical writing. There resulted manuscripts on *A Driving Guide to the Cotswolds,* several children's stories, and a family history, *Walloping Window Blind.* He is survived by his wife, Jill, a daughter, Pamela Marks, of Woodside, California, sons, John, of Issaquah, Washington, and David of Golden, Colorado, and three grandchildren. Family, friends, and colleagues remember him for his keen intellect, his sense of humor, his breadth, and his insistence on quality and high ethical standards in all organizations with which he was associated.

JOHN E. GRAY

1922–1997

BY JULIAN STEYN
SUBMITTED BY THE NAE HOME SECRETARY

JOHN EDMUND GRAY, a leading international figure in the development of nuclear power and a retired executive of numerous energy management and consulting organizations, died of a brain tumor at the home of his only daughter, Jane Redmond, in Waterville, Maine, on October 20, 1997. He had lived in Alexandria, Virginia, for the previous three decades.

John, known to close family, as Jack, one of four children, was born in Rhode Island in 1922. After high school he worked for one year at the Woonsocket Rayon Company, a local firm in the Rhode Island town where he grew up. In 1943 he earned a B.S. degree in chemical engineering from the University of Rhode Island, where he worked several campus jobs to help pay expenses.

After college John became a participant in the Manhattan Project, and during 1945 and 1946 he served in the United States Army. Between 1943 and 1960 John held the following positions: engineer with Westinghouse Research Laboratories and the General Electric Company's General Engineering and Consulting Laboratory; materials administrator, U.S. Navy Nuclear Reactors Branch; and director, Technical and Manufacturing Division of the Atomic Energy Commission's Savannah River Operations. In 1954 he became the project manager for construction of the first commercial nuclear power plant in the United States, the Shippingport Atomic Power Station in Pennsylvania.

In 1960 John entered the commercial private sector by starting up NUS Corporation (now a division of Scientech, Inc.), where he held the posts of president, chairman, and chief executive officer at various times. NUS became a consulting and engineering firm that provided energy and environment-related technical services to U.S. and foreign utility and energy companies, with the focus initially on nuclear power. During his years at NUS, he established affiliated companies in Germany and Japan, NIS GmbH and Japan NUS.

From 1972 to 1976, John served as a consultant to the Ford Foundation Energy Policy Project, the Massachusetts Institute of Technology Center for Energy Policy Alternatives, and the National Science Foundation and as the manager of the Edison Electric Institute's Nuclear Fuel Supply Study Program.

John established International Energy Associates Limited (IEAL), a Washington-based energy consulting firm, in 1975 and served as its chairman and chief executive officer until 1985, when it was acquired by ERC International, Inc. (ERCI). He served from 1985 to 1990 as president and vice-chairman of the board of directors of ERCI, and from 1988 to 1990 as chairman and chief executive officer of ERC Environmental and Energy Services. He also served as director of IEAL Energie Consult GmbH (Germany) and Evaluations Recherches Conseil (France), affiliates of ERC. He served as chairman of IEAL of Japan Company Ltd., which he cofounded in 1982, until his death in 1997.

John was recognized for his almost half century of energy development activities by his election in 1992 to the National Academy of Engineering for technical leadership in nuclear materials production, early nuclear power programs, environmental safeguards, and formulation of national energy policy. Between 1993 and 1995, he served on the Academy's Public Information Advisory Committee and the Committee on Foreign Participation in U.S. Research and Development.

John served as director and chairman of the Energy Policy Council of the Atlantic Council of the United States from 1978 until his death; and from 1985 as the Atlantic Council's vice-chairman. He served as chairman of the Council's U.S.-Japan Energy Policy Dialogue from 1980 until 1997. In 1983 he was elected a director of the U.S. Energy Association and served as its chairman between 1990 and 1992; in 1987 he was appointed the U.S. member of the World Energy Committee on Energy Issues of Developing Countries. He was a director and member of the executive council of the American Society of Macro Engineering.

John was a trustee of the Atlantic Council Foundation, the Cathedral Choral Society of Washington, D.C., and the University of Rhode Island Foundation. During the 1990s he served on the board of directors of numerous companies engaged in the energy field.

John authored, coauthored, and edited numerous books, articles, and speeches during his life in the energy business.

Energy Daily publisher, Llewellyn King said of John, "Gray was a captain of the U.S. nuclear industry, and one of the wisest and wittiest of a generation of exceptional men." Former General Dynamics chairman and chief executive officer, Hilliard Paige, described him as "an admired world leader" in the field of energy and "a class act." At John's memorial service in historic Christ Church in Alexandria, Virginia, Paige described him as "Richard the Lion Hearted, the leader of Crusades, with just enough P.T. Barnum in him." At the memorial, Joseph Harned of the Atlantic Council said, "I never met a man who could do so many things so well. He was ferocious about getting things right. And I never met anyone who was right so often." Ms. Eliane Lomax of the Atlantic Council wrote in sympathy to Jane that her father's professional life embraced "worthy goals, quality of execution, and thoughtfulness to colleagues." Ms. Lomax added, "Whenever I can, I try to pass on to those younger or less experienced the lessons in mentorship I learned from him as my way to thank and remember him."

While his "can-do" attitude and his incredible focus always impressed those who knew John in business, there was also a gentle and caring side to him. His younger son, Jeffrey, has spoken of the regular Saturday lunches he spent with his dad at the local bagel shop in the 1990s. During these sessions, Jeff said his dad would philosophize in terms like "there are no big deals," or perhaps "look to this day, for it is life," or "expect nothing and have gratitude for everything." Over the years he spent a lot of time in Japan, and had a deep appreciation for the people and the culture, and was extraordinarily well liked by friends and colleagues in that country. Again, he could be a joyous man, particularly when it came to such pleasures as sailing, and for many years he did that regularly on the Chesapeake Bay.

In another demonstration of John's caring and thoughtfulness, only a few weeks before he died he arranged with his daughter to establish a $300,000 scholarship to benefit students at the University of Rhode Island. He did so in order that they would not have to work numerous odd jobs as he had done, but could instead focus on becoming good engineers and participating in campus extracurricular life.

John is survived by his wife of forty years, Mary Lightbody Gray, who lives in Brunswick, Maine; three children, Jane E. Redmond of Waterville, Maine, John C. Gray of West Springfield, and Jeffrey N. Gray, of Fairfax, Virginia; a sister, Ruth Boyd-Horan of Wallingford, Connecticut; two brothers, Walter J. Gray of South Kingstown, Rhode Island, and Robert T. Gray of Locust Grove, Virginia; and two grandchildren, sons of his daughter Jane.

Only one month before his death, John Gray was one of ten graduates inducted into the University of Rhode Island College of Engineering's first Hall of Fame class—a fitting tribute for a truly remarkable man. The writer and his wife, Stephanie, have very fond memories of a dear friend who we feel is still with us—for the writer, a friend for more than thirty years.

RICHARD W. HAMMING

1915–1998

BY HERSCHEL H. LOOMIS AND DAVID S. POTTER

Richard Wesley Hamming, senior lecturer at the U.S. Naval Postgraduate School, died January 7, 1998, of a heart attack in Monterey, California.

Dick was born February 11, 1915, in Chicago, Illinois. His father was Dutch and ran away from home at age sixteen to fight in the Boer War. His mother's lineage goes back to the *Mayflower*. Dick went to one of the two public boys' high schools in Chicago. The family moved only once while he was growing up—to within two blocks of their first apartment.

Dick attended three junior colleges (two of those closed because of financial difficulties in the Depression.) It had been his intention to become an engineer, but his only scholarship offer came from the University of Chicago, which at that time did not offer an engineering degree. As a result he switched to mathematics, a decision he never regretted, and he received a B.S. degree in 1937. He then went to the University of Nebraska where he earned an M.A. degree in 1939, and followed that with a Ph.D. degree in mathematics from the University of Illinois in June 1942.

He met Wanda Little when she was sixteen and he twenty-one, introduced by a friend who knew they both liked to dance. Dick at this time lived at home, commuted to the University of Chicago, and studied on the "El." Wanda was then attending the only girls' high school in Chicago. Wanda received her M.S. degree (English, teaching math minor) from Illinois in June 1942. They were married in September 1942.

After marriage, both taught algebra and trigonometry at the University of Illinois to the enrollees in the Army Specialized Training Program, until February 1944. They went to the University of Louisville for a year, where Dick taught budding naval officers. Following this stint of teaching, he was invited to join the Manhattan Project at Los Alamos in April 1945. There he was assigned the task of keeping the IBM relay computers running so that the physicists could go back to working out the theoretical aspects of the atom bomb. Although Dick knew little about such machines, he learned quickly about their potential and their failings. In later interviews about these early days, he noted that even then, in spite of the primitive nature of those computers with their high relative error rates and their slow speed, they were the forerunners of tools that would lead to fundamental changes in the way science would be done in the future.

Dick left Los Alamos in 1946 to join the mathematics group at Bell Telephone Labs in Murray Hill, New Jersey. He was one of a group of talented young scientists who in their years at Bell Labs contributed greatly to extremely significant advances in computers, information theory, and of course solid-state electronics and the invention of the transistor. It was here that Dick devised an error detecting and correcting scheme now known as Hamming Codes for computers. These codes depend on the fact that in a binary code it is only necessary to know the position of a binary digit that is in error in order to correct it. To specify a particular digit in a string, say, fifty digits long requires that only six of these digits be assigned as "error correcting" positions, and the remaining forty-four become information code. The designer may go to higher levels of assurance of data integrity, the next steps being single error correction but double error identification and for more highly error prone systems, double error identification and correction. The initial *Bell System Technical Journal* article of April 1950 was used by one of us (Loomis) in a course at the University of California, Davis. "Introduction to Electrical Engineering," a course for sophomores, was designed to be motivational, and the paper was ideal because it presented a truly important result; it was self-contained, and unlike many such papers was clearly written. While still at Bell Labs, Hamming continued his work on numerical analysis, numerical integration, and numerical filtering. His major works during this period include *Introduction to Applied Numerical Analysis* (1971) and *Digital Filters* (1977).

Dick retired from Bell Labs in July 1976 and joined the faculty of the U.S. Naval Postgraduate School at Monterey, California, that same year. He had concluded that, "It was time to let the young fellows take over" and that he could best serve by teaching, writing, and "teaching future admirals how to think." Dick was concerned about retiring "too late." He did not want to overstay his welcome; he felt that "important research was done by the young" and that he should step out of the way. He taught a number of courses and wrote numerous books and articles. The essence of this part of his life was in a unique course, "Future Engineering Practice" (called affectionately "Hamming on Hamming"), and the book he wrote for it, *The Art of Doing Science and Engineering*. This course, which he taught for more than six years, was a popular elective and heavily attended. He often said, "If you don't work on important problems, it is not likely that you will do important work." He was always thinking about important problems and continually challenged colleagues and students to do the same.

One final note about this part of his life. Dick loved chocolate almost as much as he loved teaching and important ideas. A favorite quotation was written in calligraphy on his office door: "Good teachers deserve apples; great teachers deserve chocolate."

Dick Hamming was elected to the National Academy of Engineering in 1980. A partial list of other honors and prizes includes the $130,000 Eduard Rheim Award for Achievement in Technology, the Richard W. Hamming Medal created in his honor by the Institute of Electrical and Electronics Engineers (IEEE) and accompanied by a $10,000 prize, the Harold Pender Award from the Moore School of Electrical Engineering, the Turing Prize of the Association of Computing Machinery, the

Emmanuel R. Piore Award from IEEE, and election as a fellow of the IEEE. Finally, the secretary of the U.S. Navy posthumously awarded him the Navy Distinguished Public Service Award. After his death and with generous support from his widow, Mrs. Wanda Hamming, and colleagues and friends, two awards at the U.S. Naval Postgraduate School were established in his memory. The Richard Hamming Award for Interdisciplinary Achievement was first awarded in March 2000, and the Richard Hamming Award for Excellence in Teaching was awarded for the first time in September 2000.

While he was at the height of his career at Bell Labs, the Franklin Institute awarded him the Certificate of Merit for the invention and application of error-correcting codes for computer systems. The citation that went with this award is an excellent summary of the impact of Dick's work with error-correcting codes and we choose to conclude this tribute with that citation.

> Hamming's achievement enormously improved the practical application of early computers by substantially increasing their reliability. But it is even more remarkable that many modern computers still use Hamming's techniques to correct errors in main memory. Although modern computers have very reliable fundamental components, the huge number of such components, e.g. the bits in a computer's main memory, means that the probability of an erroneous result would be significant without Hamming Codes and similar codes that Hamming inspired. It is not an exaggeration to say that modern graphical computing, which requires large main memories, would be impractical without Hamming's invention. Furthermore, computers in critical control applications cannot have any significant probability of an erroneous result. These applications would not exist but for the use of the work of Richard W. Hamming.

N. Bruce Hannay

N. BRUCE HANNAY

1921–1996

BY MORRIS TANENBAUM

N. BRUCE HANNAY, retired vice-president for research and patents of Bell Laboratories and former foreign secretary of the National Academy of Engineering, died on June 2, 1996, at Harrison Memorial Hospital in Bremerton, Washington. He was a resident of Port Ludlow, Washington, where he and his wife, Joan, had lived since 1989.

Bruce was born on February 9, 1921, in Mt. Vernon, Washington, and was a descendent of early Scottish settlers in the area. He lived in Seattle until leaving for Swarthmore College, where he was elected to Phi Beta Kappa and graduated summa cum laude with a B.A. degree in chemistry in 1942. He received his M.S. and Ph.D. degrees in physical chemistry in 1943 and 1944, respectively, from Princeton University, where he studied the dipole moments of molecules with C. P. Smyth, one of the pioneers in the field. This work, during the remarkably short period of two years between his bachelor's and Ph.D. degrees, resulted in five published papers. He was also involved in the Manhattan Project during this period.

Immediately after receiving his Ph.D., Bruce joined the Research Division of Bell Laboratories and focused on the chemical and physical aspects of electronic materials and processes. His fundamental studies included thermionic emission, electron

127

attachment and ionization phenomena in molecules, and the mass spectrographic analysis of solids. The latter work led to important techniques for the identification of trace impurities in solid-state electronic materials.

In 1954 Bruce was placed in charge of a group engaged in the chemical physics of solids. This group did pioneering work on the chemical and electronic properties of semiconductors and, later, solid-state laser materials. Some of the work of this group lead to the creation of the first silicon transistors. Bruce's later research interests centered on superconductivity, and he was the first to suggest and demonstrate that intercalated (layered) compounds could be superconductors.

At Bell Laboratories Bruce rose through the research managerial ranks. He was appointed director of the Chemical Research Laboratory in 1961 and executive director, Materials Science and Engineering, in 1967. He became vice-president of Research and Patents in 1973 and retired from that position in 1982.

As foreign secretary of the National Academy of Engineering in 1976, Bruce initiated a series of studies on international competitiveness, a response to the Academy's and his own concerns about the changes in the position of the United States relative to the rest of the world, especially Japan and Europe. These changes were just becoming visible, and the work Bruce initiated was among the first to bring a bright spotlight onto the fact that our long competitive lead in technology and manufacturing had significantly shortened and, in some areas, was questionable. That stimulated other work at the National Academies and was a significant part of the activity that stimulated much introspection in industry and government and that eventually significantly improved our national competitiveness.

A prolific author, Bruce produced some eighty technical papers and authored the book *Solid State Chemistry*. He edited the book *Semiconductors,* which was one of the earliest (1959) authoritative texts devoted to the modern understanding of the chemical and physical properties of these important materials. He was the editor of the series *Treatise on Solid State Chemistry* and coeditor of the books *Electronic Materials* and *Taxation, Technology and the U.S. Economy*. He also served on the editorial boards of many of the leading solid-state journals including the *Journal of Solid State Chemistry, Materials Science and Engineering,* and *Revue de Chimie Minerale* among others.

Higher education was one of Bruce's strongest interests. He was a trustee of Clarkson College and served in advisory and visiting committee roles at many universities, including Princeton, Harvard, Yale, Brown, Caltech, Cornell, Stanford, the University of California at San Diego and at Berkeley among others. He served as Regents Professor at the University of California, Los Angeles, and the University of California, San Diego, and as the Centennial Scholar at Case Western Reserve University. He received honorary doctorates from Swarthmore, Polytechnic Institute of New York, and Tel Aviv University and the Berkeley Citation of the University of California. He was especially pleased to be instrumental in the establishment of the Bruce Hannay Fund at Swarthmore, which was recently used to endow a tenure-track position in their Department of Chemistry.

Bruce's activities in corporate, governmental, academic, and professional organizations were legion. He was a member of the boards of Rohm and Haas, General Signal, Plenum Publishing, and a family of mutual funds of Alexander Brown & Sons. He was a member of the Science and Technology Advisory Councils at Atlantic Richfield, Chrysler, Comsat, Inco, Merck, Sci/Tech Holdings, SRI, and United Technologies. He was a member of the governing board of the National Research Council (NRC), the Solid State Sciences Committee, the National Materials Advisory Board, and the Report Review Committee of the NRC, a member of the National Academy of Sciences Committee for Joint US-USSR Study of Fundamental Science Policy and the Committee for the Survey of Materials (COSMAT). He was a consultant to the National Laboratories at Brookhaven, Lawrence Livermore, and Sandia and to the Organization for Economic Cooperation and Development, International Institute for Applied Systems Analysis, and the Alexander von Humboldt Foundation. He was a frequent adviser to the White House, congressional committees, the Departments of Defense, Commerce, State, and Transportation, the Science and Technology Policy Office of the National Science Foundation, the Office of Technology Assessment, the National Bureau of Standards, and the Office of Science and Technology.

In addition to his service as foreign secretary and a member of the Council of the National Academy of Engineering, he was a member of the National Academy of Sciences, a corresponding member of the Mexican National Academy of Engineering, a fellow of the American Academy of Arts and Sciences and of the American Physical Society, president of the Electrochemical Society and of the Industrial Research Institute, chairman of the Directors of Industrial Research, a member of the board of the American Society for Testing and Materials, and a member of the American Chemical Society.

Bruce received many recognitions of his contributions, including two of the most prestigious honors for a chemist, the Perkin Medal of the Society of Chemical Industry, and the Gold Medal of the American Institute of Chemists. He was also the recipient of the Industrial Research Institute Medal, the Acheson Medal of the Electrochemical Society, and was the Monie A. Ferst Memorial Lecturer at the Georgia Institute of Technology and the Almquist Lecturer at the University of Idaho.

Bruce Hannay was a man of many talents that he devoted to his country, his profession, his company, and his family. He is survived by his wife, Joan, who continues to live in Port Ludlow, Washington, and his two daughters, Brooke Meecher of Olympia, Washington, and Robin Nelson of McLean, Virginia. He is deeply missed by all of us.

Clair A Hull

CLAIR A. HILL

1909–1998

BY BEN C. GERWICK

Cлᴀɪʀ ʜɪʟʟ, cofounder of CH2M-Hill, the internationally recognized firm of engineering consultants, died on April 11, 1998. He was eighty-eight years old.

He was born on April 20, 1909, in Redding, California. After studying forestry at Oregon State University, he graduated from Stanford University in 1934 with a degree in civil engineering.

After a brief stint with Standard Oil Company (now Chevron) and the California Department of Transportation, he returned to Redding to form his own firm, Clair A. Hill and Associates, specializing in water resources and mapping. From 1941 to 1945 he served in the U.S. Army in a bomb disposal and ordnance unit in the Aleutian Islands, returning in 1945 to reactivate his engineering firm in Redding. He became one of the principal authors of the *California Water Plan Commission* and was considered as principally responsible for its subsequent adoption and implementation. In 1971 his firm merged with CH2M to become CH2M-Hill, where he served as the California regional manager until his retirement in 1976.

Clair Hill early recognized the importance of photogrammetry and the computerized solutions to problems in water resource engineering and planning. It was his interest in water resources and agriculture that led to his proposing and developing the idea for creation of the Whiskeytown Lake Reservoir in Northern California. In 1968 Congress and the president renamed the dam

133

"The Clair A. Hill Whiskeytown Dam," a rare honor for a person still living.

Throughout his career, Clair Hill was at the heart of water planning and development in California, serving on the California Water Commission from 1949 until the mid-1990s, including a tour as chairman. He was the commission's only honorary life member.

Clair Hill received numerous awards and honors for his work in water resources, including an honorary lifetime membership in the American Society of Civil Engineers and the Association of California Water Agencies Lifetime Achievement Award. He was elected to the National Academy of Engineering in 1992.

Clair Hill enthusiastically addressed each new development that could enhance his work, learning to fly his own airplane in order to carry out his photogrammetry, and embracing geotechnical engineering when he recognized its importance in water resource engineering and irrigation.

His enthusiasm and energy propelled his firm from its start as a single person to partnership in a worldwide firm that today numbers more than 3,000 employees.

NICHOLAS J. HOFF

1906–1997

BY GEORGE S. SPRINGER

Nicholas J. Hoff, professor emeritus and former chairman, of the Department of Aeronautics and Astronautics at Stanford University, died at his home on the Stanford campus on August 4, 1997.

Nicholas was born in the small town of Magyarovar in western Hungary on January 3, 1906. At the start of the First World War, his father, a prosperous dentist, moved the family to Budapest. There Nicholas completed his secondary education at the same Evangelikus Gimnazium as Eugene Wigner, Leo Szilard, and John von Neumann. At this time he was an accomplished violinist and seriously contemplated a career in music. However, his interest in sports, especially in skiing and gliding, led him to engineering, which he studied under Aurel Stodola at the Swiss Federal Institute of Technology in Zurich.

After graduation Nicholas obtained a position at the only Hungarian airplane company at the time, the Weiss Manfred Aeroplane and Motor Works of Budapest. Here, from 1929 to 1939, Nicholas designed training planes and fighters for the Hungarian Air Force, with special interest in the airplanes' structure. In the late 1930s he contacted Stephen P. Timoshenko and asked if he could work toward a Ph.D. degree under his direction. Timoshenko accepted Nicholas as his student, and Nicholas arrived at Stanford in 1939. After receiving his Ph.D. in 1942,

Nicholas accepted a teaching position at the Polytechnic Institute in Brooklyn. There he undertook theoretical and experimental studies of the stability of monocoque-thin-walled and sandwich structures, and came up with results that are still being used to prevent buckling.

In 1957 Provost Fred Terman invited Nicholas to Stanford to start a department of aeronautical engineering. Under his leadership the department developed into one of the leading centers of aeronautics and astronautics. While at Stanford he continued his research on the stability of thin-walled structures, and in 1966, published his widely acclaimed text *Analysis of Structures*.

After he reached the mandatory retirement age in 1971, Nicholas served as a visiting professor at Rensselaer Polytechnic Institute and lectured widely in Japan, Europe, and Australia. Nicholas kept up a vigorous schedule until just a few months before his death. He swam every day and walked to the department twice a week to consult with colleagues.

Nicholas received virtually every major award in his field, including the Centennial Medal of the American Society of Mechanical Engineers (ASME) as well as the Theodore von Kármán Medal and the Worcester Reed Warner Medal of ASME. He was a recipient of the Daniel Guggenheim Medal of the American Institute of Aeronautics and Astronautics (AIAA), the Von Kármán Lecturer of the AIAA, and the Wilbur Wright Memorial Lecturer of the Royal Aeronautical Society of London. He was elected to the National Academy of Engineering in 1965, the Hungarian Academy of Science, the French Academy of Sciences, the French Academy of Air and Space, and the International Academy of Aeronautics. Nicholas was also active in several engineering societies and was a life member of the American Society of Civil Engineers, honorary fellow of AIAA, and an honorary member of ASME. He was president of the 12th International Congress of Theoretical and Applied Mechanics.

Nicholas is survived by his wife, Ruth Kleczewski Hoff, daughter-in-law, Karen Brandt of Palo Alto, and brother George Hoff of Santa Barbara.

HOYT C. HOTTEL

1903–1998

BY JÁNOS M. BEÉR, JACK B. HOWARD,
JOHN P. LONGWELL, AND ADEL F. SAROFIM

To THOSE WHO KNEW HIM, HOYT C. HOTTEL will be remembered for his intensity, intellect, and integrity. He would shut out the world as he pursued his activities, and his concentration on the problem at hand would often be mistaken for absentmindedness or aloofness. Few problems could long withstand the sustained assault of his undivided attention. His career in the Department of Chemical Engineering at the Massachusetts Institute of Technology, from 1928 until his death at the age of ninety-five on August 18, 1998, was filled with remarkable accomplishments. His final technical contribution was his narration of the history of the Combustion Institute, of which he was a cofounder, videotaped at his home on July 29, less than three weeks before his death.

He was born to Louis Weaver Hottel and Myrtle Clarke on January 15, 1903, in Salem, Indiana. His family moved shortly thereafter to St. Louis. He liked to recount, as a measure of his longevity, memories of becoming separated from his parents at the 1905 World's Fair and of watching Halley's Comet from his backyard in a St. Louis suburb. Having moved to Chicago at the age of ten, he graduated from the Hyde Park High School in 1918. He subsequently attended Indiana University, from which he graduated with a B.A. degree in chemistry in 1922.

He went directly from Indiana to MIT for graduate studies in chemical engineering and enrolled in the School of Chemical

Engineering Practice. One of the field stations of the Practice
School that he attended, first as student then as an assistant director, was the Lackawanna plant of the Bethlehem Steel Company, where he developed his lifelong interest in furnaces and
combustion. He returned to MIT to work on a doctoral thesis
on flame propagation under Robert T. Haslam. When Haslam
asked him to write up his thesis, Hottel requested that he concentrate instead on the publication of some radiation calculations that he considered to be more important. The paper he
published in *Industrial and Engineering Chemistry,* and then more
elaborately *in American Institute of Chemical Engineers (AIChE) Transactions,* in 1927 established the basis for the quantitative treatment of radiative heat transfer in furnaces and provided the transition for the treatment of radiation in furnaces from an art to a
science. This paper was the first of many digressions from writing his never-to-be-completed doctoral thesis.

Probably the most lasting of his contributions was the development of the gas emissivity charts for quantifying heat transfer
in furnaces. The sophistication of his equipment, mostly home
built, was extraordinary for any time. He designed and constructed the first infrared spectrometer at MIT and developed
such a sensitive radiometer for measuring energy fluxes that the
galvanometer would go off scale from the adiabatic temperature rise resulting from the pressure increase when the laboratory door was closed. Measurements could only be made in the
still of the early morning on days so calm that the wind would
not raise the institute flag. To eliminate interference from the
radiation of confining windows, he developed an aerodynamic
confinement of the radiating hot gas mixtures. The data that he
generated in the 1930s yielded results that provided standards
until the present. In addition to measuring gas emissivity, he
established the mathematical framework for the quantitative
treatment of furnaces and the zone method for furnace heat
transfer. He was working on a paper on his one-zone method of
analysis of furnaces at the time of his death.

Professor Hottel's other achievements include early series of
studies (1932 to 1936) of heterogeneous combustion, which first
identified quantitatively the roles of diffusion and chemical re-

action in the combustion of solid carbon. This research again reflected the sophistication of his experimental design, his meticulous attention to precision in gathering data, and his application of scientific reasoning to the interpretation of the results. One paper was reprinted fifty years later by *International Communications in Heat and Mass Transfer* as a classic contribution to the field. Some of the work was expanded by Frank Kamenetsky in his Russian book *Diffusion and Heat Transfer in Chemical Kinetics* (English publication, 1969). His ability to translate fundamentals to practice was illustrated by his application in 1941 of incorporating his single-particle models in a treatment of pulverized coal flames, which anticipated the computational treatment of pulverized coal flames to be developed three decades later.

His research on gaseous diffusion flames (1939 to 1949) provided a first quantitative treatment of the impact of transition from laminar to turbulent flows on the length of gaseous diffusion flames. As part of that research, he developed jointly with W.R. Hawthorne the concept of unmixedness. His research established the notion of the length of the flame being controlled by the mixing at a molecular level of fuel and air, and treated quantitatively the effect of unmixedness on the lengthening of the flames. These findings have become cornerstones to the understanding of turbulent flame structure.

With funding from Godfrey L. Cabot in 1938, he organized the world's first research center on the use of solar energy, a few years before the Russian heliocentric center at Tashkent. The studies led to the choice of the flat-plate collector as the most promising device for solar heating, development of the performance-predicting equations in use today for assessing such collectors and for testing new concepts, construction of the first solar-heated house and of three others that provided data for economic assessment of solar space-heating and hot water supply. Simultaneously, Professor Hottel maintained a balanced view of the significance of solar energy in national or world energy use, advocating the separation of emotional from logical inputs to the assessment of the prospects for economic use of the sun as an energy source.

During World War II, he was chief of the National Defense

Research Committee group that studied and developed incendiaries. After the war, he chaired the Armed Forces Special Weapons Panel on Thermal Radiation from 1949 to 1956. Noting that war necessitates the development of technology for ugly purposes, he turned his attention in peacetime to maximizing the contribution of the engineer and scientist to fire prevention and suppression. He was involved in organizing and chaired, for its first eleven years, the National Research Council's Commission on Physical Sciences, Mathematics, and Resources Panel for Fire Research. He was responsible for stimulating research on the reduction and suppression of peacetime fires and aided the U.S. Bureau of Standards (now the National Institute of Standards and Technology), through congressional testimony, in its successful drive to set up a fire research center.

Professor Hottel was co-founder, with Bernard Lewis and A. J. Nerad, of the Combustion Institute (International), and co-founder, with R. A. Sherman, and chairman for its first twenty-one years, of the American Flame Research Committee, subsidiary to the International Flame Foundation. Professor Hottel was elected a member of the National Academy of Sciences (1963), the National Academy of Engineering (NAE) (1974), and the American Academy of Arts and Sciences. His professional awards include the United States Medal of Merit; King's Medal for Service in the Cause of Freedom, Great Britain; Founders Award, NAE; Founders Award, AIChE; Fritz Medal, United Engineers Trustees; Sir Alfred Egerton Gold Medal, the Combustion Institute; William H. Walker Award, AIChE; Max Jakob Award, American Society of Mechanical Engineers and AIChE; ESSO Energy Award, Royal Society, London; and Melchett Medal, Institute of Fuel, Great Britain.

He was an inspiring teacher and mentor to students for more than six decades. On the principles of teaching, he said: "Beware that a student's spirit be not done to death by a formula, by teaching with answers cast in concrete. Be less concerned with technical content and timeliness of what you teach and less concerned with the completeness of coverage of your subject than with stretching the student's mind and stimulating him to self-teaching, hopefully stretched throughout life." He would often take students home to continue discussions of thesis research, and his wife, Nellie, and his four children gracefully accepted these intrusions. As one of his students recollected, he would look suddenly at his watch and exclaim, "My heavens, it's half-past six and Nellie will be wondering where I am; you'd better come home with me." Later in the evening, "My heavens, it's half past eleven. You'd better stay here tonight."

Away from academia, Professor Hottel took great pride in his extensive vegetable and flower gardens. He was a prodigious and skilled woodworker who built some beautiful hardwood coffee tables and crafted his own Christmas decorations over the years. He also built kayaks for his daughters. One of his proudest achievements was climbing Mount Teton in Wyoming with several younger MIT colleagues when he was fifty years old. He had a strong interest in classical music, and he enjoyed the Boston Symphony regularly for many years with his wife, a singer. He had a nearly perfect ear and could sing any song, using the diatonic scale. He once determined the frequency range of the sound from a research combustor at MIT by telephoning his young daughter at home and asking her to play for him the piano keys sequentially over the telephone.

He was survived by four children: Lois Hottel Wood of Lebanon, New Hampshire; H. Clarke Hottel, Jr., since deceased, of Mattapoisett, Massachusetts; Barbara Hottel Willis of Severna Park, Maryland; and Elizabeth Hottel Barrett of Annapolis, Maryland; ten grandchildren, and eighteen great grandchildren. He was a giant of twentieth century chemical engineering and leaves a rich legacy in his research output and the large number of students and colleagues, whom he inspired.

George R. Irwin

GEORGE R. IRWIN

1907–1998

BY JAMES W. DALLY

Dr. GEORGE R. IRWIN, Glenn L. Martin Professor of Engineering at the University of Maryland and professor emeritus of Lehigh University, died of congestive heart failure at his home in College Park, Maryland, on October 9, 1998. The Father of Fracture Mechanics, he was internationally known for his study of fracture and his ability to convert his scientific concepts into engineering methods applicable to a wide range of industrial applications involving a variety of structural materials.

George was born on February 26, 1907, in El Paso, Texas, son of William Rankin Irwin and Mary Ross Irwin. His family moved to Springfield, Illinois, were he attended and graduated from high school. He attended Knox College in Galesburg, Illinois, and was awarded an A.B. degree in English in 1930. He studied physics for an additional year at Knox College before transferring to the University of Illinois at Urbana. From 1931 to 1935, he was a graduate student and part-time assistant in the Physics Department at the University of Illinois. During this period in 1933, he married Georgia Shearer, who was a classmate from Knox College.

He returned to Knox College as acting assistant professor of physics, teaching there for only one year. The first of their children, Joseph Ross, was born in Galesburg, Illinois, during this year. Returning to the University of Illinois as a service fellow, he completed the requirements for a Ph.D. in 1937. His doctoral thesis was on the mass ratio of lithium isotopes.

In July 1937, George joined the staff of the U.S. Naval Research Laboratory (NRL), Washington, D.C., to lead a small group of engineers and scientists specializing in ballistics with special emphasis on projectiles penetrating targets. By the time of U.S. involvement in World War II, he had developed a straightforward but exacting technique for measuring penetration force, and its time derivative as a projectile engages a target. He personally conducted a series of penetration experiments using his new method. It was the first time in the long history of ballistics that these fundamental measurements had been made. Although this research was carried on during the war, the important work was not published until 1946 as "Penetration Resistance at Ballistic Speeds" in the *Proceedings of the Sixth Congress for Applied Mechanics.* The new experimental method enabled the Ballistic Branch at NRL, under George's direction, to develop several nonmetallic armors that were used for fragmentation protection in the Korean and Vietnam Wars.

George's interest in brittle fracture was initiated by his observation of armor plate, which chipped and cracked in a brittle manner during proof firings involving thick plates. He noted that this steel appeared to be ductile in standard Charpy impact fracture tests with small specimens. He deduced correctly that rate and size effects changed the mode of failure from ductile to brittle. He was most concerned with the gradient of the stress near a crack tip.

In 1946 George was given the responsibility for the project on brittle fracture at NRL. He changed its direction and focused on the locally concentrated stress and deformation at the crack tip. The fertility and power of this new technical approach soon became apparent. George was promoted from head of the Ballistics Branch of the NRL to associate superintendent of the Mechanics Division in 1948. Two years later, he was promoted to superintendent and served in that capacity until his retirement from government service in 1967.

The classical approach to brittle fracture in the late 1940s had been developed in the early 1920s, following the work of A. A. Griffith. Griffith had shown that an instability criterion could be derived for cracks in brittle materials based on the variation of potential energy of the structure as the crack grew. The Griffith approach was global and could not easily be extended to accommodate structures with finite geometries subjected to various types of loadings. The theory was considered to apply only to a limited class of extremely brittle materials, such as glasses or ceramics. George observed that the fracture process in metals involved nonelastic work at the crack tip. This observation permitted him to modify the Griffith theory by incorporating a plastic work of fracture in addition to the classical surface energy of crack formation.

Confusion was widespread in the literature of that era because it was not clear how a Griffith-style global energy balance related to the local physics of separation processes at the crack tip. George showed definitely in his 1950 papers that the global flux of energy to the fracture process, appearing in that overall balance, was fully explainable in terms of the locally concentrated fields of stress and deformation at the crack tip. Even more important, he showed, in the common case when the zone of nonelastic deformation occupied only a small region surrounding the crack tip, that the mathematical equations of elasticity have singular solutions for the stress fields near the tips of the cracks. These solutions were of a universal form involving a multiplying factor, now termed a "stress intensity factor" proportional to the loading. This stress intensity factor depended on the geometry of the structure and the applied loading. With these pioneering papers of the early 1950s, George had given birth to fracture mechanics.

After introducing the fundamental concept of the "stress intensity factor," which clarified the issue of fracture for the mechanics community, George moved into the materials area. He noted that the stress intensity factor could be employed as a crack tip characterizing parameter. He proposed that the conditions for the onset of crack growth could be phrased in terms of attainment of critical stress intensity factor K_{Ic}, a material property. The concept of a critical stress intensity factor is now universally accepted as a proper measure of resistance to crack growth, and rates of subcritical crack growth by fatigue and chemical attack are represented as functions of the stress intensity factor. Much of current activity developing nonlinear theory for ductile metals and polymers proceeds in a similar spirit by identifying appropriate characterizing parameters from the near crack tip singular solutions to the nonlinear continuum mechanics equations.

George recognized the huge gap between publication and practice and invested years of persistent effort needed to introduce new fracture mechanics methods to applications in industry. This was a major effort because some of the areas of structural technology had techniques that were not readily replaced. He also provided leadership and significant effort to many of the committees of the American Society for Testing and Materials (ASTM). Many of the standards developed by the ASTM committees for testing materials to establish fracture parameters are due in large part to George's work over more than two decades.

In 1967, after thirty years of service, George retired from his position as superintendent of the Mechanics Division at NRL and joined Lehigh University as the Boeing University Professor. He served on the faculty at Lehigh University for five years before reaching mandatory retirement age. During this initial period in the academic community, he interacted with many researchers and influenced their work. For example, during his tenure at Lehigh University, he influenced the work of Paul Paris in developing methods for predicting crack growth and its control in aircraft structures and of F. Erdogan on cracks in thin-walled shell structures. The list of others who either collaborated with George or were influenced by him is long. Only a few notable researchers are listed here: A. A. Wells of the British Welding Institute on characterizing fracture in normally ductile steel structures; F. A. McClintock, Massachusetts Institute of Technology, and J. W. Hutchinson, Harvard University, on the development of fracture mechanics procedures in the presence of substantial ductility; Jim Rice, Harvard University, on developing the J integral approach for characterizing the onset of crack growth in ductile materials; L. B. Freund, Brown University, and M. F. Kanninen, Southwest Research Institute, on the dynamics of inertial limited crack propagation and arrest.

After retiring for the second time from Lehigh University in 1972, George joined the faculty at the University of Maryland in College Park. I was then serving as chair of the Mechanical Engineering Department when George decided to join us. We were elated, and he formed the center of a small group, with an experimental focus, working in the area of dynamic fracture. At that time we were concerned with crack arrest and its implications in a loss-of-coolant accident of a nuclear reactor. With his guidance we were able to establish a measure of crack arrest toughness and to develop a test standard for its measurement in tough reactor-grade steels.

The list of honors bestowed on George is long, but they all are worthy of recognition.

1946   Naval Distinguished Civilian Service Award
1947   Knox College Alumni Achievement Award
1959   ASTM Charles B. Dudley Medal
1960   RESA Award for Applied Research
1961   Ford Foundation Visiting Professorship, University of Illinois
1966   ASTM Award of Merit
1966   American Society of Mechanical Engineers (ASME) Thurston Lecture
1967   Fellow, ASTM
1969   University of Illinois Engineering Achievement Award
1969   U.S. Navy Conrad Award
1969   Alumni Achievement Award, University of Illinois
1973   SESA Murray Lectureship Award
1974   Lehigh University Academic Leadership Award
1974   ASTM honorary member
1974   American Society for Metals Sauveur Award
1976   The Grande Medaille Award of the French Metallurgical Society of France
1977   ASME Nadai Award
1977   B. J. Lazan Award from the Society for Experimental Mechanics
1977   Honorary degree, doctor of engineering, Lehigh University

1977   Election to the National Academy of Engineering
1978   ASTM-Irwin Award
1979   Francis J. Clamer Clauier Medal of the Franklin
        Institute
1982   Governor's Citation for Distinguished Service to Mary-
        land
1982   Tetmajer Award of the Technical University of Vienna,
        Austria
1985   Fellow, Society for Experimental Mechanics
1986   ASME Timoshenko Medal
1987   ASM Gold Medal for Outstanding Contributions to
        Engineering and Science
1987   Elected to foreign membership, British Royal Society
1988   ASTM Fracture Mechanics Award and the George R.
        Irwin Medal
1989   Honorary membership in Deutscher Verband für
        Material Prufung
1990   Honorary membership in the American Ceramic
        Society
1990   Albert Sauveur Lecture Award
1992   George R. Irwin Research Award, University of Mary-
        land
1993   Engineering Innovation Hall of Fame at the Univer-
        sity of Maryland
1998   A. James Clark Outstanding Commitment Award
        University of Maryland
1998   Appointed Glenn L. Martin Institute Professor of
        Engineering

George is survived by his wife, Georgia Shearer Irwin, of Col-
lege Park, Maryland; four children, Mary Susan Gillett of
Dunkirk, Maryland, Sarah Lofgren of Berwyn Heights, Maryland,
Joseph R. Irwin of Seabrook, Maryland, and John S. Irwin of
Raleigh, North Carolina; ten grandchildren and four great-grand-
children.

George will long be remembered by all of us in the engineering profession as a remarkable engineer and scientist. But I will
remember George more as a gentle man than an outstanding

engineer. He had so much character it is impossible to describe. He was never assuming or presumptuous. Many men of achievement become filled with themselves. Not George R. Irwin—he remained humble in spite of his long list of awards and accolades. He sought no glory or legacy. He shared his ideas and was pleased to see others develop his initial concepts. Our research group often gathered in his office to discuss our ongoing work in the dynamics of fracture—I will always remember his quiet ability to keep us on track and to guide us through difficulties. We will sorely miss him.

Burgess H. Jennings

BURGESS H. JENNINGS

1903–1996

BY MORRIS E. FINE AND HERBERT S. CHENG

Burgess hill jennings, professor emeritus of mechanical engineering at Northwestern University, passed away June 6, 1996, at Raleigh, North Carolina, where he moved after a long and distinguished career in academic research, teaching, and administration. His specialty was environmental engineering, particularly, heating, cooling, and ventilating.

Burgess was born September 12, 1903, in Baltimore, Maryland, the son of Henry Hill and Martha Burgess Jennings. Educated at the Johns Hopkins University and Lehigh University, where he was also a faculty member, he joined the faculty of the new Northwestern Technological Institute in 1940 as professor of mechanical engineering, and in 1943 became chairman of the department. He took leave in 1957 as director of research for the American Society of Heating, Refrigerating, and Air-Conditioning Engineers. He resumed his faculty position at Northwestern University in 1960, taking on the added duties of associate dean of the Technological Institute for Research and Graduate Studies, a position he held until his retirement in 1970. He continued his engineering activities at Northwestern for many years after retirement, consulting for U.S. government agencies, universities, and corporations on energy use, power, environment control, and education.

The outstanding engineering accomplishments of Professor Jennings are evidenced by his authorship of many textbooks not only in heating and air conditioning, refrigeration, and environmental engineering, but also in other areas including steam and gas engineering, internal combustion engines, gas turbines, and gas dynamics. They have made a substantial impact on mechanical engineering education because they have been and are still widely used by engineers and students around the world. A large number of his students are leaders of industry, responsible engineering educators, and administrators. His research and papers on absorption (heat-operated) refrigeration were significant in advancing this type of cooling at a time when compression refrigeration was predominant.

Among many contributions made by Professor Jennings to engineering was the extended consultation service he provided to the kitchens of Sara Lee from 1961 to 1972 in energy use and refrigeration. These efforts led to the development of the technology and practice now associated with the wide distribution of frozen bakery products.

Professor Jennings was extremely active in professional society activities. He served as treasurer, vice-president, president, and director of research of the American Society of Heating, Refrigeration, and Air-Conditioning Engineers (ASHRAE). He was a founder and also served as secretary and then vice-president of the Society of Tribologists and Lubrication Engineers (formerly known as American Society of Lubrication Engineers).

Professor Jennings was elected to the National Academy of Engineering in 1977. He was cited for distinguished contributions to engineering education, research, and practice, and energy use to improve man's welfare and environment. Burgess received many other awards. He was a fellow and honorary member of the American Society of Mechanical Engineers (ASME). He won the Richards Memorial Award from ASME in 1950 as "the most outstanding mechanical engineer twenty-five years after graduation"; the Worcester Reed Warner Medal of ASME in 1972 for "significant contributions to permanent literature in engineering"; and the F. Paul Anderson Medal of ASHRAE in 1981 "for contributions to energy usage and human welfare."

His research contributions were primarily in refrigeration and solar energy as an alternative energy source for cooling as well as heating. He is author or coauthor of more than 100 papers and articles.

Robert A. Laudise

ROBERT A. LAUDISE

1930–1998

BY JOHN J. GILMAN

AN ICON FOR CRYSTAL GROWTH TECHNOLOGY and a strong advocate for materials technology in general, Bob Laudise is greatly missed by the community in which he worked, as well as the community of his family and his personal friends. His professional skills created an impressive legacy of technical landmarks as well as some new and permanent institutions. His humanity and gentle humor are irreplaceable in the memories of his colleagues and family members.

I first met him during a visit to Bell Telephone Laboratories. I was a grower of metal crystals; he of oxides. In particular, he was in the midst of developing the hydrothermal process for producing quartz crystals on an industrial scale for use to control the frequencies of electrical oscillators. I was impressed by his intelligence, his enthusiasm for the task at hand, and his pride in what had already been accomplished. Only a few years beyond graduate school, he had accepted responsibility for a difficult task and was executing it with skill. I was delighted later on when he contributed two chapters to a book that I edited, called *The Art and Science of Growing Crystals* (1963). His own very successful book, *The Growth of Single Crystals* (1970), was published a few years later.

Robert Laudise was born to Anthony T. Laudise and Harriette E. (O'Neil) in upstate New York in the town of Amsterdam along

159

the Mohawk River. This was not far upstream from the place where he began his career training in chemistry at Union College in Schenectady, the home base of the General Electric Company at the time. He graduated from Union College in 1952 with a B.Sc. degree and traveled east to the Massachusetts Institute of Technology, where he studied inorganic chemistry and received a Ph.D. degree four years later in 1956.

A major step came next when he was hired by AT&T Bell Laboratories (now part of Lucent Technologies). Unlike many others, he never left, and became highly valued by the management. In fact, he was so highly valued that a special position was made for him toward the end of his career so he was not required to retire when he reached the mandatory retirement age. He was still "in harness" as adjunct chemical director at the time of his death, August 20, 1998.

Starting in 1956 as a member of the technical staff at Bell Laboratories, Robert Laudise rose through the ranks. In 1970 he became the head of the Crystal Chemistry Research Department, followed two years later by a promotion to the position of assistant director and then director of the Materials Research Laboratory. In 1978 he became director of materials and processing research. After he reached the retirement age of sixty-five, he was appointed adjunct chemical director.

The approach of Laudise to crystal growth was systematic. It was that of a careful physical chemist and a disciplined chemical engineer. This was essential to the development of an industrial-scale hydrothermal process for making quartz crystals. It was also important for guiding the efforts of his group in developing the workhorse among solid-state lasers, the neodymium yttrium-aluminum garnet (Nd:YAG), and the workhorse of nonlinear optical-frequency convertors, lithium niobate crystals.

His responsibilities were not limited to crystal growth, his first love, but included other aspects of the synthesis of new materials. A significant example is his supervision of the development of processes for the production of optical fibers on a commercial scale.

Robert Laudise was a tireless advocate of the technology of crystal growth as a free-standing discipline—in other words, a branch of chemical engineering. He used both social organizations and publications to promote his advocacy.

Together with Kenneth A. Jackson, he started the American Association for Crystal Growth (AACG) and worked hard to build it into a stable and effective nationwide organization. As a member of the New Jersey Chapter, I attended a number of the local meetings, spoke before one or two of them, and read the AACG Newsletter with interest for several years. Later, this organization combined with a group of European crystal growers to become the International Organization of Crystal Growth, the IOCG.

In the words of Kenneth Jackson, "One of the prime motivations for starting the AACG, in addition to establishing a forum where we could assemble to interchange our news and views on the subject, was to promote crystal growth and to provide an identity for our field. In this, Bob had a special talent, and he was effective and successful at improving our image in the scientific community and the world at large."

After the *Journal of Crystal Growth* began publication in 1967 under the founding editor, M. Scheiber, Laudise became one of the editors in 1974 and continued in that capacity, or as an adviser, until 1998.

As his career progressed, Robert Laudise's professional interests broadened. The group of people under his supervision worked on an increasingly large variety of materials, using a great variety of techniques. The properties they were interested in were primarily electronic and optical. The scope did not include metallic, polymeric, or other structural crystals, but within the scope there was great variety.

As a spokesman for crystal growth and the behavior of materials more generally, Laudise was an active participant in the pertinent professional societies both as a member and in various officiating positions. He was a past president of the American Association for Crystal Growth as well as the International Organization of Crystal Growth. In addition he was a past chairman of the Solid State Chemistry Subdivision of the American Chemical Society. The American Association for the Advancement of Science elected him as a fellow, as did the American

Mineralogical Society. Other professional societies of which he was a member were the Institute of Electrical and Electronics Engineers (senior member), American Ceramic Society (fellow), Sigma Xi, Electrochemical Society, Materials Research Society (founding member), Federation of Materials Societies (president), and American Philosophical Society.

Many people receive prizes for their professional work, but few have prizes named for them. In the present case, the International Organization of Crystal Growth established the Laudise Prize in 1989. Other prizes awarded to Robert Laudise were the Sawyer Prize, 1976; A.D. Little Fellow (MIT), 1976; IOCG Crystal Growth Prize, 1984; *Industrial Research Magazine's* IR-100, 1989; American Chemical Society's Materials Chemistry Prize, 1990; Orton Award of the American Ceramic Society, 1994; Applications to Practice Award of the Materials Society, 1995; 200th Anniversary Medal of Union College, 1995; Past President's Award of the Federation of Materials Societies, 1998; and the Eitel Award for Excellence in Silicate Science from the American Ceramics Society, 1996. Robert Laudise was elected to the National Academy of Engineering in 1980 and to the National Academy of Sciences in 1991.

Many advisory committees benefited from Laudise's expertise. Some of the committees he advised, together with some of his other professional activities, were as follows:

- U.S. President's Science Advisory Committee, 1970
- Advisory Committee to the National Bureau of Standards (NIST), 1970 to 1980; and 1986
- Advisory Committee to the National Aeronautics & Space Administration (NASA), 1975 to 1980
- National Academy of Sciences–NASA Evaluation Committee, 1980
- National Research Council's (NRC) joint Engineering and Technical Systems National Materials Advisory Board and Physical Sciences, Mathematics, and Resources Solid State Sciences Committee Panel on Materials Research Opportunities and Needs in Materials Science and Engineering, member from 1985 to 1993

- Committee on Scholarly Exchange with China (PRC), 1980 to 1998
- NRC Commission on Engineering and Technical Systems National Materials Advisory Board, member from 1987 to 1998
- Editorial Advisory Board of the Journal of Materials Science, 1988 to 1998
- Solid State Sciences Committee (NAS), 1980 to 1985
- Visiting committees: Materials Processing Center (MIT), 1987 to 1998
  - Alabama A&M Physics Department, 1985 to 1998
  - University of Wisconsin Materials Department, 1989 to 1998
  - Oak Ridge National Laboratory, 1989 to 1998

He made many contributions to the literature of materials science and technology. He also was the author (or coauthor) of fourteen U.S. patents and 160 technical papers. For some fourteen years, he was the North American editor of the *Journal of Crystal Growth*. He was also editor of the *Journal of Materials Research*.

Influences of technological activities on environments, and ecologies, became a major interest of Robert Laudise in the latter part of his career. He was active in encouraging AT&T to establish Industrial Ecology Faculty Fellowships, a grant to develop the *Journal of Industrial Ecology*, and conferences on industrial ecology. These conferences allowed practitioners to meet to exchange knowledge and engage in policy discussions. He believed that well-implemented industrial ecology should pay for itself and provide competitive advantage to those practicing it.

HANS LIST

1896–1996

BY GORDON H. MILLAR

In SEPTEMBER OF 1996, DR. HANS LIST, elected as a foreign associate of the National Academy of Engineering in 1989, died at age 100. At the time of his passing, he was the only member of the Academy of that mature age. Dr. List was born on April 30, 1896, in the year when Rudolf Diesel presented his plans for a new internal combustion engine that was then named after him.

As a boy Hans List showed a great promise as a musician and could easily have pursued a career in music as an accomplished artist on both the piano and the cello. His technical instincts, however, were far too strong and he gave up a promising career in music to pursue engineering and science.

While working on new diesel engine technology in the Johann Weitzer Wagon and Machine factory, List wrote his doctoral dissertation on "The Regulation of Diesel Engines." It was quite unusual in those days that someone would write a thesis without academic supervision, especially since he had used mathematical methods that could not be verified with a slide rule. His thesis had to be given to a very strict mathematician but was approved with excellent results. It was rather typical for Hans List that one day in 1924, he asked his parents to come to a ceremony at the Technical University in which, to his parents' surprise, he was awarded a Ph.D.

In the late 1920s, List saw an ad in a German technical journal for a lecturer in internal combustion engines at a Chinese university. He applied and shortly moved to China, an adventurous undertaking. The Tongji University in Woosung near Shanghai had been founded by Germans, and the language of instruction was German. The engine laboratory was well equipped, and List could conduct a number of experiments and tests. He witnessed the Chinese Civil War, the conflict between the North and South, and the growing tension between China and Japan.

After six years, Hans List was offered a professorship at the Department of Thermodynamics and Internal Combustion Engines at the Technical University of Graz, Austria, and he accepted. During the following years, he worked together with his assistants who later became colleagues in his engineering office on diesel engines and the gasification of solid fuels. During that time he also started work on the publication of a 14-volume standard reference work, *The International Combustion Engines.* Its updated version is still the basic course book for mechanical engineering students in Europe. His last volume was published in April 1996.

The research facilities in Graz were modest. Therefore, Hans List responded to an invitation to succeed the famous Professor Naegel, an acknowledged master of diesel engine research at the Technical University of Dresden. Apart from teaching, Professor List carried out research on the construction of aircraft engines and published numerous papers. He set up an office in Vilsiburg, Bavaria, and cooperated with well-known companies, such as Daimler-Benz and Bayrische Motorenwerke. After eyewitnessing the horrible air raid that devastated Dresden, Hans List moved to Vilsiburg where he continued his research on piston engines and aircraft turbines.

After World War II, List returned to Graz and founded an engineering office—AVL—together with four of his former colleagues from the Technical University of Graz. He received financial assistance from the Marshall Plan and was able to expand his business. List paid back the Marshall Plan loan in full not many years after starting his company. Few loan recipients did this well. His first big contract with the Jenbacher Werke provided the financial background for the further development of his company. In the years that followed, the rapidly expanding and practice-oriented research institute designed and developed numerous engines for tractors, trains, vessels, and aircraft. Today the company has business relationships with most automobile manufacturers of the world.

In the 1960s Hans List planned and built an engine factory in Egypt. The factory was completed in less than three years and still exists today. A similar concept was developed for a factory in Korea. He continued throughout his career to build international business relationships overseas and in many European countries.

It was clear to Hans List that, in the future, improvements would be necessary and environmental constraints would be placed on engines. One problem was noise, and Professor List set out to find ways to reduce noise. Over the years, AVL branched out into other important fields: instrumentation and engine testing. Today AVL is not only a leader in engine testing and engine test equipment, but has also specialized in the field of medical instruments. Ninety-eight percent of AVL equipment is produced for export. To comply with the ever-increasing environmental requirements, AVL has concentrated its work on meeting the strictest emission requirements and has become a highly regarded specialist in this field.

Hans List managed his privately owned research institute for many years, and in 1979 handed over management to his son, Helmut. He had visions of the future throughout his life and was able to realize many of his ideas. He was an example to his staff for living what he said and thought and was an example of self-discipline and willpower. Even at the age of 100, he came to his office daily, climbed the stairs to the second floor, and spent his days thinking of how to improve the diesel engine, a model of which he kept on his desk. He registered his latest patent at age ninety-eight, a record that was entered in the *Guinness Book of Records*. Dr. List was awarded an astonishing 364 patents.

Hans List set an example by establishing a business in the second half of his life, at an age when many people can think only of retirement. Those who spoke of him did so in respectful, admiring terms. Attendees to the company ball held in his honor on June 14, 1996, were impressed when he opened the gala waltzing with Kathryn Millar List, his daughter-in-law.

Howard Lomax

HARVARD LOMAX

1922–1999

BY RICHARD A. SEEBASS

H<small>ARVARD LOMAX</small>, a research fellow and senior staff scientist at the National Aeronautics and Space Administration (NASA) Ames Research Center and consulting professor at Stanford University, died on May 1, 1999. He was a gentle and quiet man who provided many significant advances in aerodynamics and fluid mechanics through his deep knowledge of mathematics and computers, his remarkable inventiveness, his dogged diligence, and his persuasive technical leadership.

Harvard was born in Broken Bow, Nebraska, on April 18, 1922. In 1940, when he had graduated from high school, his aunt, Edith Stephenson, encouraged him to move to California, which he did. For a while he made her San Francisco home his California headquarters. She encouraged his study at Stanford, where he thought he might become a writer. She was more practical and realized his talent was in mathematics. Soon he was studying mechanical engineering at Stanford. While there, he met Joan Whitmore, who received her degree in social science and psychology. They were married December 31, 1943. With a subsequent master's degree in music, Joan taught both piano and music at DeAnza College, where she conducted the senior citizen chorus for over twenty years. They had three children, Harvard Laird (1945), James Whitmore (1948), and Melinda (1959).

Graduating from Stanford Phi Beta Kappa in mechanical engineering in 1944, Harvard was soon in the U.S. Navy and assigned to Moffett Field as an engineer. The only course he had found difficult at Stanford was machine shop. Nevertheless, the Navy made him a research scientist in a 16-foot high-speed (for that time, but less than Mach 1) wind tunnel. His theoretical ability soon made it evident that Harvard should join the National Advisory Committee on Aeronautics Ames Theoretical Aerodynamics Branch under Dr. Max Heaslet. In this branch, Harvard soon made many important contributions, including a little-known but extraordinarily informative derivation of the supersonic area rule [NACA RM A55A18]. He understood the hyperbolic equivalent of the Green's function for elliptic equations, i.e., Riemann function, which he used to derive the supersonic area rule. This derivation made it clear how to separate wave drag due to lift from that due to volume, and thereby how to minimize the wave drag for a given lift and volume (or maximum cross-sectional area). Subsequently, Harvard's results were widely used throughout the industry. This culminated almost twenty-five years of theoretical aerodynamics research, which for most would be a career in itself. But Harvard's career was far from over. The age of the "numerical wind tunnel" was on the horizon, and Harvard was among the first to see its potential.

In 1958 the NACA became NASA with both aeronautics and space in its charter. In an effort to speed up the reduction of data from their wind tunnels, NASA Ames arranged for the purchase of its first computers in the late 1950s. This attracted Harvard's attention, and he soon learned machine language to be able to evaluate the results from his theories. The Theoretical Aerodynamics Branch was subsequently used to educate others at Ames, by their rotation through this branch, in the use of computers and computational methods.

With the arrival of transistorized computers and FORTRAN, Harvard began a long career devoted to the development of computer methods for the solution of aerodynamic problems. Hans Mark, NASA Ames, and Dean Chapman, division chief for thermo- and gas-dynamics, wisely decided to form a Computational Fluid Dynamics (CFD) Branch with Harvard as its chief, and with Robert MacCormack as assistant chief. This talented group made rapid advances with the arrival of a CDC 7600 in early 1970s. In 1972 the Illiac IV arrived. This was the first serious parallel computer. Despite this group's talent and Harvard's own diligence, it took nearly four years to make the Illiac IV operational.

To allow Harvard's CFD group to focus on the fundamentals of the computational methods, as well as on improving computing speed, a new branch was formed for Applied Computational Aerodynamics. This focus on the fundamental issue of "getting the physics right," which is most difficult in turbulent flows, continues to pay handsome dividends even today in our growing knowledge of turbulent flows through the joint NASA Ames–Stanford Center for Turbulence Research.

Despite their struggles with the Illiac IV, the branch, and soon the center were focused on procuring a special-purpose computer for fluid dynamic flows. This they called the Numerical Aerodynamic Simulator Program (NASP). In the formative stages of the NASP, a group of us advised the Ames management that everything about NASP seemed sound, except the program should purchase the best available computers for its needs, rather than trying to have a special-purpose computer developed for them. Whether this advice was correct is not known, but NASP, with Harvard as it father, became the Numerical Aerodynamic Simulator Facility.

This facility made many important contributions to computer technology, computational methods, and the simulation of aerodynamic propulsive flows. It provided an ever-improving "numerical wind tunnel" and made many important contributions to aerodynamic and propulsion technology for commercial and military aircraft. It was Harvard Lomax who not only saw that this could be, but in large measure was personally responsible for making it happen.

Among the many awards Harvard received were the NASA Medal for Exceptional Scientific Achievement in 1973, the American Institute of Aeronautics and Astronautics (AIAA) Fluid and Plasma-Dynamics Award in 1977, and the Presidential Rank Award for Meritorious Executive Service in 1983. He was elected

an AIAA fellow in 1978 and a member of the National Academy
of Engineering in 1987. He received the Prandtl Ring in 1996.

All who knew Harvard admired his gentle ways, his extraordinary mathematical talents, his kind humor, and his quiet but
effective leadership. This "gentle giant" is sorely missed.

Albert G. Mumma

ALBERT G. MUMMA

1906–1997

BY DAVID S. POTTER

REAR ADMIRAL ALBERT G. MUMMA, U.S. Navy (retired), died July 15, 1997, in Philadelphia, Pennsylvania. Funeral services were held in the Naval Academy Chapel, followed by interment in the Naval Academy Cemetery with full military honors.

Admiral Mumma was born on June 2, 1906, in Findlay, Ohio. He was a member of a family with an outstanding military tradition. His father, Colonel Morton G. Mumma, was a graduate of the U.S. Military Academy, class of 1900. His two brothers, Rear Admiral Morton C. Mumma, Jr., and Major George E. Mumma, were both graduates of the Naval Academy.

Admiral Mumma received his early education at Army posts in Iowa, Texas, the Philippines, and Washington, D.C. After graduation from Iowa High School in Iowa City in 1922, he entered the U.S. Naval Academy with a congressional appointment from Iowa.

He was a member of the rifle team and also a midshipman battalion officer while at Annapolis. He graduated with distinction, eighteenth in a class of 456. He also received the award established by the class of 1924 for highest standing in the graduating class for the course in the Department of Engineering and Aeronautics. During 1932 to 1934 he continued his education with a course in naval engineering at the Naval Postgraduate School of the Naval Academy. He also attended the L'Ecole d'Application du Genie Maritime in Paris from 1934 to 1936.

Sea duty during his early naval career included service aboard the USS *Richmond*; the USS *Seattle,* flagship of the United States fleet, in 1927; and the USS *Saratoga,* the first U.S. carrier, during her fitting-out period and later commissioning until June 1931. In 1936, on completion of his studies, he was assigned the post of chief engineer of a new destroyer leader, the USS *Clark* (DD361).

During World War II he served on the staff of the commander of Naval forces in Europe and also the Alsos Mission (European technical intelligence) mostly in France with the Army. It was in connection with this work that he headed the technical group visiting the headquarters of Admiral Doenitz at Flensburg and Glucksburg, Germany, just before VE-Day. This activity secured Dr. Helmuth Walter and his coworkers, who had been involved in a number of weapon systems for the Germans. This was the start of the extensive evaluation of the technology of the German wartime projects.

He returned to the United States after the war and in December 1945 became deputy director of ship design for the Bureau of Ships, Navy Department. He was also designated as deputy coordinator of nuclear matters and head of the Nuclear Ship Propulsion Program until 1948. He was production officer at the San Francisco Naval Shipyard from 1949 to 1951. He was promoted to rear admiral in 1954 and commanded the Mare Island Naval Shipyard, which was being converted to nuclear-powered submarine construction. Finally, he became chief of the Bureau of Ships in 1955. This was the period of rapid conversion to nuclear power plants for naval ships and a time of great change.

In June 1959, immediately after his retirement from the United States Navy, he joined Worthington Corporation as vice-president of engineering. In 1962 he was elected to the board of directors. He was rapidly promoted to executive vice-president in 1964 and president in April 1967. In November 1967, he was elected chairman of the Worthington Corporation. He served in this capacity until retirement in July 1971.

Admiral Mumma was a past president and honorary member of the American Society of Naval Engineers as well as past president and fellow of the Society of Naval Architects and Marine Engineers. He received the Admiral Jerry Land Gold Medal given by the latter society for contributions to naval architecture. He was elected to the National Academy of Engineering in 1976 and served on several committees of the National Research Council. He held the degree of honorary doctor of engineering, awarded by Newark College of Engineering. In 1971 he was appointed by President Nixon to chair the American Shipbuilding Commission to study and report on measures to improve the shipbuilding posture of the U.S. Navy and the Merchant Marine. This task involved considerable interaction with the civilian and military leadership of the Navy. In addition to receiving a number of U.S. decorations, he was knighted by the Queen of the Netherlands and holds the Order of Knight Grand Officer of Orange Nassau.

Admiral Mumma was a director of a number of financial and industrial organizations. Chief among them were directorships in the Prudential Insurance Company of America, the C. R. Bard Corporation, and Kueffel and Esser Company. He was also active in community service, particularly education. He served as a trustee of the Webb Institute of Naval Architecture, Drew University, and the St. Barnabas Hospital in Livingston, New Jersey.

Admiral Mumma served his country well through his noteworthy career in the U.S. Navy and his work in guiding the activities of the American Shipbuilding Commission. In addition to being a knowledgeable leader and colleague, he was also a pleasure to work with.

Ryoichi Nakagawa

RYOICHI NAKAGAWA

1913–1998

BY TREVOR O. JONES

DR. RYOICHI NAKAGAWA, retired executive managing director, Nissan Motor Company, Ltd., died in Tokyo, Japan, on July 30, 1998. Dr. Nakagawa was born in Tokyo on April 27, 1913, and received his B.Sc. degree in mechanical engineering and his Ph.D. in engineering from the prestigious University of Tokyo. Not only was Dr. Nakagawa one of the nicest and kindliest people I have ever met, but he was also one of the most aristocratic. My wife and I fondly remember Dr. Nakagawa coming to our home in Birmingham, Michigan, and spending a lot of time with our children teaching them origami and Japanese children's games. This no doubt had an influence on our daughter, Bronwyn, who majored in Japanese at the University of Michigan.

Although I originally met Dr. Nakagawa through our mutual interests in automobile design, we both came from the aerospace and defense industries. It was through these earlier defense-related experiences that we calmly discussed the implications of the United States dropping the two atom bombs on Japan. Our discussions were both interesting and objective and, most important, each of us understood the other's position.

Dr. Nakagawa devoted his sixty-year career to engineering in a wide array of disciplines. He started his career as an aircraft engine designer in 1936 at Nakajima Aircraft Company and stayed at this company until the end of World War II.

Like me, Dr. Nakagawa transitioned from the aerospace and defense industry to the automotive industry. Dr. Nakagawa was executive managing director of Prince Motor Company in 1964 when it merged with Nissan Motor Company and he became managing director and subsequently executive managing director.

Dr. Nakagawa was a leading force in Japan in bringing aerospace technology to the automobile. To memorialize this transition, Dr. Nakagawa wrote a paper, "From Aircraft to Automobiles—Memories of an Engine Designer," which was published in the *Journal of the Japan Society of Mechanical Engineers* in 1982. One of the areas of major importance was electronics. In this regard, he was fully aware of the limitations of electromechanical control systems. Dr. Nakagawa fully embraced this challenge and started Japan Electronics Control Systems Company, Ltd. (JECS) to design, develop, and manufacture automotive electronic control systems. JECS was a subsidiary of Nissan and was a joint venture with other automotive electronics suppliers. I visited JECS with Dr. Nakagawa, and he was very proud of his new company; he said to me, "Jones-San, you recommended we have our own Delco Electronics Company and here it is." As a result of this in-house automotive electronics capability, Dr. Nakagawa led Nissan and JECS in developing pioneering emission control systems, fuel injection systems, and many other advanced automotive electronic systems.

Dr. Nakagawa had immense credibility in the engineering community, as demonstrated by an enormous amount of recognition. He was a foreign associate of the U.S. National Academy of Engineering and a member of the Engineering Academy of Japan. He was president of the Society of Automotive Engineers of Japan and a recipient of the Japanese Government's Third Order of the Sacred Treasure and Blue Ribbon Medal, the Merit Medal for Army Technology of the Japanese Department of the Army, the Progress Award of the Imperial Society of Inventors, and the Transportation Cultural Award from the Japanese Department of Transportation.

Throughout his career, Dr. Nakagawa was a prolific author, inventor, and keynote speaker. He received his first patent in

1942 on fuel injection systems for aircraft engines and successfully carried this technology into the automobile.

Dr. Nakagawa was a renaissance person in advancing harmony
between industries and nations. Perhaps the following recommendations by one of his references for membership in the
National Academy of Engineering exemplifies this:

> Dr. Nakagawa has been a pioneer in stimulating new ways
> of working together between industries and governments.
> Particularly noteworthy is his leadership in establishing and
> helping to manage the cooperative activity that was car-
> ried out by the members of the Japanese automotive in-
> dustry, members of the U.S. petroleum industry, and Ford
> Motor Company through the Inter-Industry Emission Con-
> trol program. This program was particularly important in
> bringing together and rationalizing diverse views that ex-
> isted among those industries involved in the early efforts
> to reduce automotive emissions. Dr. Nakagawa was an ef-
> fective spokesman and advocate for the Japanese industry.
> He was particularly effective in developing a relationship
> with U.S. industry members that led to greatly improving
> understanding and trust on the part of all participants in
> the program. The acknowledged success of this program
> was due in large measure to the efforts and leadership of
> Dr. Nakagawa.
>
> Dr. Nakagawa's involvement in automotive engineering, his
> directorship of the electronic activity of Nissan Motor Com-
> pany, and his continuing involvement in the university sys-
> tem in Japan is a clear measure to his broad interests and
> the concern that he has for the impact of engineering on
> related areas.

As one of Dr. Nakagawa's closest friends in the United States,
I had the true privilege to support his nomination for membership in the National Academy of Engineering. I know his knowledge, presence, and ever-smiling and welcoming face will be
missed by all whom had the good fortune to meet him.

KENNETH D. NICHOLS

1907–2000

BY JOHN W. SIMPSON

GENERAL KENNETH DAVID NICHOLS was born in Cleveland, Ohio, in 1907. He entered West Point in 1925 and was graduated fifth in his class of 1929, receiving a B.S. degree.

He reported to Fort Humphreys (now Fort Belvoir), Virginia, on September 13, 1929, as a second lieutenant in the U.S. Corps of Engineers and was assigned to the U.S. Army Engineer Battalion in Nicaragua for survey work on the proposed Nicaraguan Inter-Oceanic Canal. He was awarded the Nicaraguan Medal of Merit for work done after the Managua earthquake in March 1931.

General Nichols attended Cornell University from July 1931 to June 1933 and received the degrees of civil engineer and master of civil engineering. He reported to Vicksburg as assistant director of the U.S. Waterways Experiment Station. This station was engaged primarily in experimental work in conjunction with flood control on the Mississippi River and with river and harbor responsibility of the U.S. Army Corps of Engineers.

In 1932 he married Jacqueline Darrieulat. They had two children, Jacqueline Ann and Kenneth David, Jr.

In 1934 to 1935, on orders from the War Department, General Nichols attended the Technische Hochschule, Charlottenburg, Berlin, Germany, under a fellowship of the Institute of International Education, established for the purpose of studying European hydraulic research methods. There followed successive tours of duty at Vicksburg; the State University of Iowa, where he received a Ph.D. degree in hydraulic engineering; Fort Belvoir; and West Point, where he served four years as an instructor in the Department of Civil and Military Engineering at the U.S. Military Academy.

After leaving West Point in 1941, General Nichols served as area engineer in charge of construction of the Rome Air Depot, Rome, New York, and the Pennsylvania Ordnance Works at Williamsport.

In July 1942 General Nichols was selected for assignment to a special corps of engineers organization set up in the summer of 1942 by President Franklin D. Roosevelt for developing and producing the atomic bomb. This project became known as the Manhattan Engineer District, and General Nichols was initially assigned as deputy district engineer and subsequently in August 1943, as district engineer. In this capacity, General Nichols supervised the research and development connected with—and the design, construction, and operation of all plants required for—the production of plutonium and uranium-235, including the construction of the towns of Oak Ridge, Tennessee, and Richland, Washington. His office at Oak Ridge became the administrative center of the wartime atomic energy activities. The project involved the expenditure of approximately two billion dollars.

The district engineer to whom General Nichols reported directly was General Leslie R. Groves, commanding general of the Manhattan Project. General Nichols continued to serve with the Manhattan District until the responsibilities for atomic energy were turned over to the United States Atomic Energy Commission in January 1947. At that time, he was appointed professor of mechanics at the United States Military Academy at West Point, New York. Although this was intended to be a permanent appointment, the pressure of atomic energy work first required his service as a consultant to the U.S. delegation to the United Nations Atomic Energy Commission and to the Military Liaison Committee to the U.S. Atomic Energy Commission. Early in 1948, with the increase in international tension, he was relieved from duty at West Point, promoted to the grade of major general, and assigned as chief of the Armed Forces Special Weapons Project. This project was a joint Army-Navy-Air Force command charged with atomic weapon logistical training responsibilities. He served as chief of this project from 1948 until January 1951. During the same period, he was deputy director for Atomic Energy Matters, Plans, and Operations Division of the general staff of the U.S. Army and was senior army member of the Military Liaison Committee to the U.S. Atomic Energy Commission (AEC).

In the fall of 1950, when Mr. K. T. Keller was appointed director of guided missiles for the Department of Defense, General Nichols was assigned as deputy director of guided missiles and was the principal assistant to Mr. Keller in discharging his responsibilities for advising and assisting the secretary of defense in the research and development and production of Army, Navy, and Air Force guided missiles. He continued to serve with Mr. Keller until the completion of his assignment in September 1953.

In January 1952 the Army reorganized its research and development activities. At that time, General Nichols was appointed chief of research and development, U.S. Army, in addition to his other duties as deputy director of guided missiles.

On October 31, 1953, General Nichols retired from the Army in order to accept appointment as general manager of the U.S. Atomic Energy Commission. During his tenure, the AEC started the nuclear reactor demonstration program, which led to the building of five types of experimental reactors. At this time the AEC was involved in the controversy over J. Robert Oppenheimer, the nuclear physicist who directed the development of the first atomic bomb. Oppenheimer was dropped as a consultant to the AEC and stripped of his security clearance after he was accused of being a security risk. General Nichols resigned from this post in April 1955 and, as a registered professional engineer in the state of Maryland, worked as a consulting engineer in the fields of research and development and commercial atomic power. His consulting firm was retained for various lengths of time by the following organizations: the Aluminum Company of America, the Carborundum Company; Koppers Company, Inc.; Gulf Oil Corporation; Westinghouse Electric Corporation; Detroit Edison

Company; Yankee Atomic Electric Company; Firestone Tire and
Rubber Company; Edison Electric Institute; Aerojet-General
Corporation; Chas. T. Main; Inca; Panama Canal Company; the
U.S. Atomic Energy Commission; Consolidation Coal Company;
the U.S. Army Corps of Engineers; and the Electric Power Re-
search Institute. He was an associate of the Overseas Advisory
Associates, Inc.

General Nichols was a director of the Detroit Edison Company, Fruehauf Corporation, and Callery Chemical Company,
chairman of the board of Westinghouse International Atomic
Power Company Ltd. (Geneva, Switzerland), chairman of the
board of Westinghouse Nadge Associates, a director and vice-
president of the Army Distaff Foundation, a member of the Secretary of the Army's Scientific Advisory Panel, a member of the
Permanent International Commission of the Permanent International Association of Navigation Congresses, a member of the
Advisory Board of Directors of the Association of the U.S. Army,
and a trustee of the Thomas Alva Edison Foundation. He served
as a member-at-large, Division of Engineering and Industrial
Research of the National Research Council; as a member of the
Advisory Committee on Civil Defense of the National Research
Council; as a member of the Project Committee of the National
Academy of Engineering; as a member of the Advisory Committee to the Department of Housing and Urban Development of
the National Academies of Sciences and Engineering. In the field
of nuclear power, he served as a member of the Committee of
the Atomic Industrial Forum Study of the Cost and Price Structure for Enriched Uranium. For the Atomic Industrial Forum,
he chaired the Study Committee on Uranium Enrichment Services Criteria and Projected Charges in 1965 and the Study Committee on Private Ownership and Operation of Uranium Enrichment Facilities in 1968. He was a member of the Steering
Group of the Ad Hoc Senior Management Uranium Enrichment
Policy Committee for the Atomic Industrial Forum Uranium,
Enrichment Report in 1972.

General Nichols was a member of the National Academy of
Engineering and the West Point Society of the District of Columbia, a fellow of the American Nuclear Society, and an honor-

ary member of the American Society of Mechanical Engineers. He was awarded the U.S. Distinguished Service Medal (Oak Leaf Cluster), the U.S. Atomic Energy Commission's Distinguished Service Award, the Most Excellent Order of the British Empire (Degree of Commander), and the Collingwood Prize (American Society of Civil Engineers). In 1984 he received the Chiefs of Engineers Award for outstanding public service.

In 1987 General Nichols completed his personal account of how America's nuclear policies were made. His book, entitled *The Road to Trinity*, was published by William Morrow and Company.

In June 1990 General and Mrs. Nichols moved from their farm near Sugar Loaf Mountain, Maryland, where they had lived for more than twenty years. General Nichols died of respiratory failure on February 21, 2000, at the age of ninety-three. At the time of his death, he lived at the Brighton Gardens retirement home in Bethesda, Maryland. Survivors include his wife, Jacqueline, of Bethesda; their daughter, Jacqueline Anne Thompson of Bethesda, and their son, Kenneth David Nichols, Jr., of Olympia, Washington; and four grandchildren, Catherine Anne Nichols, Kenneth David Nichols III, Nicole Therese Thompson, and Anthony J. Thompson, Jr.

FRANKLIN F. OFFNER

1911–1999

BY ALVIN M. WEINBERG AND PETER J. DALLOS

F RANK OFFNER was our colleague, collaborator, and friend. He was also a bona fide genius. It is usually straightforward to give a eulogy. One addresses scientific achievements, honors, and accomplishments and then says what a nice person the departed was. Our task is not so simple—which Frank Offner shall we talk about? Frank the scientist, the inventor, the industrialist, the teacher, or the artist?

Frank was fond of telling stories about his childhood, which according to all accounts, was a happy one. Frank was born in 1911. As a youngster, he was mostly interested in things mechanical, and he guarded the carpenter tools he received at age seven until his sons appropriated them much later. He turned to electronics at age eleven, when he received his first crystal radio. The early infatuation with radios lasted through his teen years, but it was interspersed with a developing fondness for chemistry and near misses of blowing up his home chemistry laboratory. He had excellent science teachers at Milwaukee University School, and they encouraged his obvious talent and native curiosity.

He studied chemistry at Cornell University, but he apparently spent more time on ham radio than in chemistry labs. To understand more about radios, Frank started to concentrate on physics. He also moonlighted in various physics labs, where he began his career as an electronic instrument designer. He graduated from Cornell University in 1933 with a bachelor's degree in chemistry and went on to Caltech, where he obtained a master's degree in 1934 in physical chemistry under Linus Pauling. As Frank was fond of telling, the Caltech education was spectacular and set him up for life with a basic background in physics, upon which much of his later success was built. He excelled among his fellows, passing his qualifying exams with the highest grade and impressing Pauling with his ingenious solution to his master's thesis problem.

Frank wanted to continue toward a doctorate in theoretical chemistry, but could not financially afford to stay at Caltech. Instead, he secured a small stipend in the physics Ph.D. program at the University of Chicago. While taking courses, he also developed a reputation as the resident electronics expert, and people came to him with problems to solve from all over campus. Eventually he was offered a technician's job in the laboratory of Ralph Gerard, an early pioneer of bioelectricity. Frank designed and built amplifiers, which allowed them to view on primitive oscilloscopes action potentials in the frog's sciatic nerve. As Frank told it later: viewing these nerve spikes changed his life's work. He would unravel the mystery of the action potential. That is when he decided to become a biophysicist. Gerard wanted to study the then newly discovered electroencephalogram. To understand this complex signal, it was insufficient simply to view it on the oscilloscope. One needed a permanent record. Frank constructed the world's first direct-writing oscillograph, using a piezo-crystal to move the pen and thereby achieving excellent frequency response. Soon after this, to enable the recording of EEGs from several electrodes, he constructed the world's first differential amplifier. The direct-writing oscillograph, equipped with differential amplifiers, was the forerunner of virtually all contemporary EEG and EKG machines. Frank built many of these and eventually licensed his invention of the portable EKG machine to a commercial company for manufacturing.

Meanwhile, there was also thesis work to do. Under the direction of Carl Eckart, in collaboration with Alvin Weinberg and Gale Young, Frank developed a mathematical model of nerve conduction. The model assumed that an electrical resistance change should accompany the nerve impulse. Such was actually measured in the squid axon by Cole and Curtis in the same year. The theory was published in 1940 and was a starting point for the most influential theory and model in all neuroscience, the Hodgkin/Huxley model of the nerve impulse.

After receiving a Ph.D. in 1938, Frank, with some encouragement from potential customers and with the sum of $500, started Offner Electronics. One of his first projects was the design of an EKG machine to monitor and transmit cardiac electric signals from a free-falling parachutist to ground observers. This was probably the first telemetered biological data. By this time World War II was in full force and Frank wanted to offer his talents to the war effort. He established a long and successful relationship with Hamilton Standard, where he solved the problem of measuring vibrations of propellers. This was necessary to help compensate for these vibrations, and the results hugely advanced propeller design and the success of our aircraft in World War II. Among the many war projects for which he was responsible are infrared missile guidance systems and heat-homing glide bombs, electronic fuel controls for jet engines, and the phase synchronizer for multipropeller planes. Offner Electronics also built many of the scalers, or Geiger counter circuits, used in the Manhattan Project.

After the war, Offner and Offner Electronics returned to the manufacture of EEG recorders. After the invention of the transistor in 1952, Frank was among the first to see its extraordinary potential in electronic circuits, and by 1956 the first transistorized EEG machine was on the market. This, the Type R Dynograph, became the world standard. That year was actually the most important in Frank's life, for on a business trip to Europe he met and later married his wife, Janine. In 1961 Offner Electronics merged with Beckman Instruments, and Frank began working for the combined outfit. The working styles of Arnold Beckman and Frank Offner were too different for the partnership to last, and in 1963 Frank left industry. He became a professor of biophysics at Northwestern University in the Electrical Engineering Department, where, until he achieved emeritus status some twenty-five years later, he was paid $1 a year.

At Northwestern, Frank continued his exploration of membrane biophysics, publishing a number of models for bioelectric membrane processes; all based on his exquisite understanding of physics and chemistry. Because of the highly mathematical and complex nature of his work, Frank often encountered difficulties with journal reviewers and editors. All of us had occasion to listen to him rail about some poor, stupid soul who couldn't solve a differential equation if his life depended on it, yet stood in judgment over Frank's latest intellectual offspring. During the last few years of his active career, he became interested in the auditory system, and one of us worked on several projects together with him.

While there were some difficulties in disseminating his written work, there were also signs of recognition of his extraordinary contributions. Among these were fellowship in the Institute of Electrical and Electronics Engineers and the receipt of the Institute's Centennial Medal. He was also a Laureate in Technology of the Lincoln Academy of Illinois, a recipient of the Professional Achievement Citation from the Alumni Association of the University of Chicago, and a member of the National Academy of Engineering. And with more than sixty patents, many papers and books, and fresh ideas daily, Frank influenced those of us lucky enough to interact with him. But his influence extends to many others—there is hardly a research lab or hospital lab in the world that does not make use of equipment that can be traced to Offner. Every time you fly on a jet plane, it is the successors of his controllers that keep the engines humming. When you are on a multiengine prop plane, it is his synchronizers that allow the plane to fly smoothly. We hope you don't fire any heat-seeking missiles, but if you do . . . remember Frank.

JOHN R. PHILIP

1927–1999

BY SHLOMO P. NEUMAN

JOHN ROBERT PHILIP, Australia's most distinguished environmental physicist and mathematician, was struck by a car and killed in Amsterdam on June 26, 1999. The accident happened while John was on his way to deliver a series of scientific lectures in the United States, following a two-week sojourn at the Centre for Mathematics and Computer Science in Amsterdam and an earlier visit to Ben Gurion University in Israel.

John was born at Ballarat in rural Victoria on January 18, 1927. His father was a dairy inspector and his mother a teacher and Methodist lay preacher. From his father he drew a passionate enthusiasm for Australian Rule football and cricket; from his mother, a lifelong love of learning and a knowledge of the Bible. Yet at age thirteen, John rose and left an evangelical service, declaring himself agnostic. He was supported in this act of defiance by Frances Julia Long, his wife-to-be.

John displayed prodigious mathematical talent at an early age and won an open scholarship to Scotch College (high school) in Melbourne, his ticket out of depression era rural poverty. There he was encouraged to write poetry, which remained a lifetime avocation and appeared in numerous literary publications as well as the standard collection of Australian verse. John matriculated at fifteen to enter Queens College at the University of Melbourne. At nineteen he received a bachelor's degree in civil engineering, an experience he described later as "very ordinary indeed," its "take home" message having been that "all things are understood, and all a young engineer needs to know is what handbook to use."

John was appointed by the university as graduate assistant in agricultural engineering and was seconded to the Commonwealth Scientific and Industrial Research (later to become Commonwealth Scientific and Industrial Research Organization [CSIRO]) Irrigation Research Station in Griffith. Here he discovered that, to agricultural scientists struggling to deal with the hydraulics of furrow irrigation, all things were not understood and there was no handbook with ready answers. It was up to John to deploy a then-limited armory of mathematical tools, coupled with his acute physical insight, to start identifying and eventually solving a vast array of unresolved problems concerning the movement of water, energy, solutes, and gases through the natural environment of soils, plants, and the atmosphere. In John's recent words, "I blundered into a line of work that has turned out, over the past fifty years, to be more fun than work."

John's funding ran out after a year and he joined the Queensland Water Supply Commission as an engineer responsible for design of irrigation supply canals. At that time he married Frances and, together with her, developed strong links to the world of art and ideas. When he left the commission, a letter of reference extolled John's engineering talents but cautioned about his bohemian appearance and behavior. Despite this cautionary note, the impact of John's work earned him a research contract at the CSIRO Division of Plant Industry at Deniliquin, New South Wales. He took up his position in 1951. Due to an acute postwar housing shortage, the newlyweds had to live in a tent on the banks of the Edwards River. John's time in Deniliquin was remarkably creative and set the scene for much of his future work.

At age twenty-six, John proposed to the CSIRO a major and unique initiative in integrated land and water research, for which there was no parallel elsewhere. It took the organization more than forty years to partially implement this remarkably farsighted vision.

A month after John joined CSIRO, Otto Frankel (later Sir Otto), a distinguished plant geneticist, was charged with revitalizing the then-somewhat moribund division. On the advice of Professors John Jaeger and Pat Moran of the Australian National University, Otto freed John to pursue independent research in agricultural physics. John set out to develop a mathematically rigorous theory of water movement and heat flow in shallow agricultural soils. One of his first and most important achievements was the development of an equation for the rate at which water seeps into a partially saturated soil, now widely known as the Philip infiltration model. This and related work earned him a D.Sc. in physics from the University of Melbourne in 1960, followed by an honorary D.Eng.

In 1959 John became head of the Agricultural Physics Section of Plant Industry and moved to Canberra in 1964. There he assembled a team of researchers to work on fluid mechanics of porous media, micrometeorology, plant physical ecology, and soil physics. A bequest to the CSIRO provided funds for the F.C. Pye Laboratory, designed by Ken Woolley, whose frugal elegance fosters scientific interaction and accommodates a multiplicity of functions. The group became the Division of Environmental Mechanics in 1970, with John Philip as chief. He occupied this position for twenty years. He took on additional administrative responsibilities as director of the CSIRO Institute of Physical Sciences. In a report drafted to the Royal Commission on Australian Government Administration, John championed scientific autonomy by describing the necessary environment for effective and creative scientific research. It is now a minor classic in the field.

Though he retired to become the first CSIRO fellow emeritus in 1992, John continued to do full-time research at CSIRO Land and Water in Canberra, producing a substantial body of new work each year.

John's rich scientific oeuvre includes major contributions to the understanding and analysis of multiphase flow and energy transport in porous media. He laid the mathematical foundations for the physics of water flow and heat transfer in unsaturated soils. He developed seminal theories and engineering approximations for water infiltration into unsaturated soils, thermally induced water movement in porous media, flow and volume change in swelling soils, mechanics of electrical double layers, hydrodynamic stability of fluid interfaces, capillary condensation and physical absorption, flow of non-Newtonian liquids in porous media, pollution of groundwater by hydrocarbons, and water flow around subterranean cavities. John pioneered the concept of soil-plant-atmosphere as a thermodynamic continuum for water transfer and developed theories of heat and mass transfer within vegetation canopies, dynamics of osmotic cells, and diffusion of tissue turgor in physiology. In addition, he studied diurnal and annual water cycles as well as annual cycles of carbon dioxide sublimation and condensation on Mars. His contributions are summarized in more than 300 skillfully crafted scientific papers that are models of brevity and precision. In some, the gap between two equations represents many days of work. Editors and reviewers who had the temerity to recommend changes received short shrift. Those who could not follow his mathematics were beyond the pale.

John's prolific solutions to a wide range of fundamental and applied problems of environmental science have made him a world-renowned and honoured authority on porous media and the soil-plant-atmosphere system. The powerful influence and great originality of John's work are reflected in more than 4,500 citations at his death.

John was a fellow of the Australian Academy of Science, the Royal Society of London, the Royal Meteorological Society, and the Soil Science Society of America. He was a foreign member of the All-Union (now Russian) Academy of Agricultural Sciences, and the second Australian foreign associate of the U.S. National Academy of Engineering. He was the recipient of the 1995 International Hydrology Prize. In 1998 he was made an officer of the Order of Australia for "services to the science of hydrology." One prize he appreciated enormously was the Jaeger Medal of the Australian Academy of Science, awarded to him in April 1999. John Jaeger was John's only and highly influential scientific mentor.

John Philip is survived by his wife, Frances, a notable Australian painter; their adult sons, Peregrine and Julian; and daughter, Candida.

This memorial draws freely on obituaries written by Stephen J. Burges (Department of Civil and Environmental Engineering, University of Washington, Seattle), Phillip W. Ford (CSIRO Land and Water, Canberra, Australia), and Ian White (Centre for Resource and Environmental Studies, Australian National University, Canberra, Australia).

OTTO H. SCHMITT

1913–1998

BY HERMAN P. SCHWAN AND DAVID B. GESELOWITZ

O‍TTO HERBERT SCHMITT died on January 7, 1998, in Minneapolis three months shy of his eighty-fifth birthday. Otto will be remembered for his scientific contributions to biophysics and biomedical engineering, for the crucial role he played in the establishment of these fields, and as a great inventor.

Otto was born in St. Louis, Missouri, on April 6, 1913. He obtained his B.A. degree at Washington University (St. Louis) in 1934 and his Ph.D. degree in physics and zoology in 1937. He was a National Research Council Fellow and Sir Halley Stewart Fellow at the University College in London during 1938 and 1939. During the war he served as a research engineer at Columbia (1942 to 1943) and supervising engineer, Special Devices Division, Airborne Instruments Laboratory (1943 to 1947). He joined the University of Minnesota, Minneapolis, as an instructor of physics and zoology in 1939. He retired in 1983 as professor of biophysics, biomedical engineering, and electrical engineering, although he continued to teach and work in his laboratory.

Otto was a leader of the emerging fields of biomedical engineering and biophysics. His interests covered many fields. His broad orientation was largely due to his inquisitive mind and his education, which was unusually diversified. Another important influence was his admired older brother, Frank Schmitt, an outstanding neuroscientist whose work was also broadly oriented. But most of all, he depended on his wife, Viola, whom he married in 1937 and who preceded him in death after a marriage of fifty-eight years. Viola was always at his side. She kept order in his incredible productivity. He was deeply in sorrow after her death.

One of us (Herman P. Schwan) met Otto for the first time at a meeting of the American Physiological Society in Columbus in 1950. Herman was actively involved in a multisociety group responsible for planning the first interdisciplinary annual conferences concerned with engineering in medicine and biology. The annual conferences had started three years earlier and were primarily oriented toward x-ray technology and medical physics concerned with ionizing radiation. The attendance was poor and without perceptible growth. Reorientation toward medical electronics, electrophysiology, and biological impedance work was indicated. Otto Schmitt agreed to organize the eleventh annual conference. The meeting in Minneapolis was on computers in medicine and biology. It was a great success and nearly 400 persons attended. From then on things moved rapidly, ensuring a good future for the interdisciplinary field.

About 1955 Otto and Herman attended a meeting at the Mayo Clinic concerned with potential hazards caused by microwave exposure. They discussed the need for a biophysical society. A few years later the first meeting of the Biophysical Society took place, organized by the "committee of four," including Kacy Cole, E. Pollard, O. Schmitt, and S. Talbot. A few years later the Biomedical Engineering Society was formed, and Otto served as the initial caretaker president.

Otto told David B. Geselowitz that as a youngster he built a Tesla coil but found that the available current from the local transformer was inadequate. Complaints to the power company were of no avail. So he inductively shorted the circuit at the fuse box, and the transformer burst into flames and was immediately replaced with one of higher capacity. At one point, his mother walked in while he was experimenting with the Tesla coil. Sparks were shooting from her son's mouth and ears, and she fainted. In high school Otto rewired a motor used by a teacher to demonstrate the effect of load on a dc motor. When the teacher grabbed the motor to apply a load, the motor increased its torque throwing the teacher off the podium.

From 1931 (when he was eighteen years old) to 1939, Otto published some seventeen articles in the *Review of Scientific Instruments* and the *Journal of Scientific Instruments* describing a series of inventions, many of which are of exceptional importance. In 1934 he patented the idea of using a pentode as the plate resistor for a pentode, thus achieving a much higher gain. Otto told David B. Geselowitz that RCA infringed on the patent, but when his attorney approached RCA, he was advised to sue. The cost ($20,000) of such an action was prohibitive. Otto was bitter and did not patent many subsequent devices, which included the cathode follower, the differential amplifier, the chopper-stabilized amplifier, and the Schmitt trigger. During the Second World War he made important contributions, which were top secret. One of his inventions was a magnetic anomaly detector to pinpoint the presence of enemy submarines.

Otto was an excellent engineer and biologist. The "Schmitt trigger" is an electronic circuit that produces an output when the input exceeds a predetermined threshold; it still appears in hundreds of applications. It is an excellent example of "bionumetics," a term that Otto coined for a field that applies biological design principles to engineering. His work in the well-known laboratory of Bernhard Katz in London and his participation in the Cold Spring Harbor Symposia brought Otto in early contact with many leading electrophysiologists. His work with Airborne Instruments Laboratories on Long Island during the 1940s contributed to the development of his outstanding engineering talents.

A few examples will serve to illustrate his wide-ranging interests. Shortly after the war he constructed an automatic instrument that could evaluate nerve preparations and could rapidly determine its cable properties on-line. He used the instrument to study and publish on the topic of dynamic negative admittance components in statically stable membranes. He and John J. Almasi constructed a highly precise impedance-measuring instrument that extended the frequency range down to a few millihertz and provided very high resolution. It was a forerunner of the precision impedance analyzers to come. He also could not help but become interested in the debates about bioeffects of weak electric and magnetic fields. So he and Robert D. Tucker worked on the perception of magnetic fields. This work was quoted often to demonstrate the extent to which one must be willing to go to exclude spurious confounding effects (in their case, minute and weak vibrations of the magnets).

After the war Otto turned his attention to the relationship between cardiac sources and the surface electrocardiogram. His laboratory was one of four that contributed to this effort to understand the volume conductor problem, and led to the development of lead systems for determining the heart vector. The others were Burger in Utrecht, Frank in Philadelphia, and McFee in Ann Arbor.

One of us (David B. Geselowitz) got to know Otto well when we served together on an advisory board established by Hubert Pipberger in 1962 in connection with his efforts to develop a system for computer interpretation of the electrocardiogram. We also served on the American Heart Association Committee on Electrocardiography, which developed standards for electrocardiographs, addressing such issues as frequency response and electric safety. Otto's suggestions were always insightful.

It was at this time that David became aware of a game that Otto played. Often when he had an idea to propose, he couched it in obscure language. On many occasions he propounded these ideas to people who nodded politely without having any idea of what Otto was saying. When Otto was challenged to explain what he meant, he would rephrase his idea in a more intelligible form. When an understandable statement emerged, it was almost invariably a solid idea. Otto frequently offered ideas to others to develop.

Otto believed in redundancy. He always carried about a dozen pens, no two of the same model to avoid simultaneous failures. He always seemed to be able to fish out from one of his innumerable pockets a gadget someone needed at the moment. He had several working tie clips, including one with a slide rule, one with an abacus, and one with a gun that could be charged with gunpowder. On several occasions he brought dead silence to a large gathering by firing the gun.

The tremendous range of Otto's contributions is not easy to convey. It is best illustrated by a topical list indicated by his publications, his biography, and our personal experience: Nerve impulse mechanisms, tridimensional oscilloscopic displays, bivalent computers; biological tissue impedance analyses; electronic circuitry; direct current transformers; trigger circuits; electronic plethysmography; antenna radiation pattern measurements; stereovector-electrocardiography; phase space displays; bioastronautics; electromagneto-biology; technical optimization of biomedical communication and control systems, Santosh Index for quality of life, strand epidemiology, personally portable whole life medical history, and biomimetic science and technology.

Otto was widely recognized for his outstanding achievements. He was elected to the National Academy of Engineering in 1979 and to the Minnesota Hall of Fame in 1978. Among his other honors are the Lovelace Award, 1960; the William J. Morlock Memorial Award, 1963; the John Price Wetherill Medal, 1972; the Institute of Electrical and Electronics Engineers EMBS Career Achievement Award, 1987 and 1963; and the Medical Alley Award, 1988.

Otto seemed to us to have an unlimited amount of energy and never grew tired of lively discussions. He also loved to laugh at others and himself and was always ready to tell great stories. Whenever he visited he offered to demonstrate a new gadget, which he had acquired. Otto had a wonderful mind, combining extensive knowledge with insight, originality, and humor. We met him for the last time at the fall meeting of the National Academy of Engineering four or five years ago and we spent a few hours together. He told Herman that his wife, Viola, was not well and it was obvious that he was worried. He was rather lonely after the death of Viola. We understand that his mind never gave up.

JUDITH A. SCHWAN

1925–1996

BY LEO J. THOMAS

J UDITH A. SCHWAN, for thirty-seven years a driving force in the development of new photographic products and an early example for her colleagues of how much women could contribute to the engineering profession and to the management of technology, died on March 19, 1996, at the age of seventy. Her entire working career was spent at Eastman Kodak Company, where she retired in 1987 as assistant director of the worldwide Kodak Research and Development Laboratories.

Judy was born in Middleport, New York, on April 16, 1925. After graduating from high school, she worked for a year as a billing clerk long enough to know she wanted a greater challenge. She wanted to attend college—she had an early interest in science and said she might have become a high school science teacher. However, World War II changed the landscape. Engineering schools were looking for female students to fill the places normally occupied by men. In 1943 she enrolled in the five-year chemical engineering program at the University of Cincinnati. Upon graduating, she was admitted to the graduate college at Cornell University. By that time, many veterans were returning from the war and resuming their chemical engineering education, and there was a paucity of openings in the engineering school. So Judy majored in chemistry, receiving her master's degree in physical chemistry in 1950. Even though her advanced degree was in chemistry, she had taken mostly chemical engineering courses. She said she favored engineering because she liked to make things work and to see how they came out.

Judy joined the Kodak Research Laboratories in 1950 as a research chemist; she began in the Emulsion Research Division, which was the inner sanctum of Kodak research at that time. There was still a lot of "art" in adapting photographic science to the creation of new products, and she quickly made her mark applying engineering thinking to this task. She was awarded more than twenty-one patents from her personal research efforts. These research contributions included improvement in color reproduction by extending the spectral sensitivity of color film; stabilizers and accelerators for color processing; increased light-recording sensitivity of silver halide emulsion; and better signal-to-noise performance in color films. But her major impact came from her leadership in developing new products such as Kodachrome II, Kodachrome 64, Kodacolor II, Kodacolor 400, Ektachrome 400, and Eastman color motion picture products. For her contributions to the movies, she was awarded the Herbert T. Kalmus Memorial Award by the Society of Motion Picture Engineers in 1979.

She rose steadily in her management responsibilities from senior chemist to laboratory head in 1965. In 1968 she was appointed assistant director of the Emulsion Research Division and director of the division in 1971. In 1975 she was appointed assistant director of the Kodak Research Laboratories. Her efforts to open the channels of communication from the inner sanctum of trade secrets to the broader Kodak research community were important to the productivity of the company.

As a research manager she set an example for hard work, rarely arriving at the labs later than 6:15 A.M. Still she had time to become an excellent golfer. She was decisive, tough (some said blunt), but always fair and good-humored. As a woman in a corporate engineering environment, she earned her promotions in the more difficult days before the gender barriers began to come down for women at Kodak. She was a role model and mentor, an effective but nonstrident feminist, and a career counselor for both men and women.

She was elected to the National Academy of Engineering in 1982. Among her other honors was the Distinguished Alumnus Award of the College of Engineering of the University of Cincinnati, and the Athena Award of the Rochester, New York, Chamber of Commerce.

She served for many years on the board of trustees of St. John Fisher College and was a member of the executive committee of that board. She was elected to the council of the Industrial Research Institute and served from 1979 to 1981. She was a member of the Society of Motion Picture and Television Engineers, the American Chemical Society, and the Society of Photographic Scientists and Engineers. Judy's church was an important part of her life, and she served her Catholic parish and diocese in a number of lay positions.

She is survived by two sisters, Jane Hirschbeck and Rosemary Trump, and is fondly remembered by her friends and colleagues.

Joseph F. Shea

JOSEPH F. SHEA

1926–1999

BY GEORGE E. MUELLER

JOSEPH F. SHEA, senior vice-president for engineering at Raytheon Company, and former manager of the Apollo Spacecraft Program Office at the National Aeronautics and Space Administration, died at his home in Weston, Massachusetts, on February 14, 1999.

Joe was one of the great systems engineers of our time and one of my personal heroes. He was a brilliant engineer, a great leader, an outstanding manager, an inspired speaker, and a great intellect. One of his many contributions to Apollo was the decision to base the mission on rendezvousing in lunar orbit. This decision was central to a successful lunar landing in the decade, and it is a tribute to Joe's logic and leadership that he was able to build a consensus among the three space centers, Marshall Space Flight Center, Cape Canaveral, and Johnson Space Center, at a time when they never agreed on anything.

Joe was born in the Bronx, New York, on September 5, 1926. He served in the U.S. Navy from 1944 to 1947 and was commissioned an ensign in 1946. He was a graduate of the University of Michigan, where he earned bachelor's degrees in engineering and mathematics, and a master's degree and a doctorate in engineering mechanics. He also taught at the university from 1949 to 1950 and again from 1953 to 1955.

From 1955 through 1959, Joe was a military development engineer at Bell Telephone Labs in Whippany, New Jersey. In that position he was intimately involved in direction of the project that led to the development of the extremely accurate radio-inertial guidance system employed in the Titan I intercontinental ballistic missile. He contributed a considerable amount of engineering innovation and project management skill and was directly responsible for the successful development of this pioneering guidance system.

From 1959 through 1961 as director of advanced research and development and program manager of the inertial guidance system development project for the Titan II ICMB, Joe was responsible for a number of significant engineering achievements, in particular the introduction of then-new technology relating to the design and development of solid-state power generation systems in long-life operational guidance equipment. This feature was a major factor in the reliability and continuing readiness of the still-operational Titan II ballistic missile weapon system, which is a major element of the current strategic deterrent missile force in the United States.

Joe joined Space Technology Labs in 1961 and while there directed advanced systems analysis and preliminary design studies of classified, advanced-technology ballistic missile defense concepts.

In 1962 Joe joined NASA and at first had the systems responsibility for Apollo and later became the project manager at the Manned Spacecraft Center for both the capsule and the lunar module. He was responsible for the definition of the basic design concept for the Apollo lunar landing mission, including the Apollo spacecraft command and service modules and the lunar module. He was the chief engineer of the design and development effort for lunar spacecraft, and directed the extensive spacecraft test and evaluation program. Joe directed the initial Apollo conceptual studies, which established the technical feasibility and advantages of the Lunar Orbit Rendezvous technique, which had a major impact on the ability to achieve the Apollo objectives on-schedule and with minimum development and mission risk. He directed the spacecraft development program through the most critical development phases. He contributed personally and directly by making key decisions regarding engineering and scientific applications, and actively directed the critical system tradeoffs and integration among spacecraft development, flight crew operations, and overall Apollo flight operations.

At NASA, Joe made outstanding contributions to the establishment of the basic Apollo lunar mission concept, and he directed the initial design, development, and test of the Apollo spacecraft command and service modules. His technical skills and managerial abilities contributed in a significant way to the final successful achievement of our national goal of landing men on the Moon and return them safely to Earth before the end of the decade of the 1960s.

In 1967 and 1968 Joe held the position of vice-president of engineering for the Polaroid Corporation in Cambridge, Massachusetts. In 1969 Joe joined Raytheon as senior vice-president of engineering and was responsible for all engineering and technology developments as well as all quality-assurance programs.

Joe continued his public service activities after having entered the private sector. He chaired a task force established by NASA Administrator Daniel S. Goldin in 1993 to review plans for the Hubble Space Telescope servicing mission and the Defense Science Board Task Force on Countermeasures and Defense Suppression and served as a member of the Division on Engineering and Physical Sciences Aeronautics and Space Engineering Board of the National Research Council. In 1964 Joe received the Arthur S. Flemming Award as one of the ten outstanding young men in government for directing the studies that led to the selection of lunar orbit rendezvous as the mission mode for the Apollo moon landings. The Massachusetts Institute of Technology named Joe the 1989 Jerome C. Hunsaker Visiting Professor of Aeronautics and Astronautics.

Joe was the recipient of numerous honors and awards. He was elected as a member of the National Academy of Engineering in 1971 and was a fellow of the American Institute of Aeronautics and Astronautics and of the American Astronautical Society.

Joe is survived by his wife, Carol; five daughters, Mary S. Helt of Framingham, Massachusetts, Nancy C. Shea of Denver, Colorado, Patricia A. Cash of South Yarmouth, Massachusetts, Amy V. Shea of Acton, Massachusetts, and Hilary Shea Crowley of Weston, Massachusetts; a son, Joseph E. Manion of Framingham, Massachusetts; a sister, Jeanne Tombini of New Rochelle, New York; a brother, Gerald Shea of Middletown, Maryland; six grandchildren; and one great-grandchild.

ROBERT S. SILVER

1913–1997

BY MYRON TRIBUS

ROBERT SIMPSON SILVER, James Watt Professor of Engineering, Glasgow University, emeritus, died at a nursing home in Inverurie, Aberdeenshire, Scotland, on April 21, 1997.

Bob was born in 1913 in Montrose, where his family had a laundry business. He studied natural philosophy at Glasgow University, where he received his M.A. and B.Sc. degrees (1st Class Honors). He continued his studies for the Ph.D., specializing in gaseous combustion.

During World War II his major work at G. & J. Weir Ltd. was with the Admiralty, improving warship pumps, boilers, and the small onboard immersed-tube desalinators. He had a long career in research and development, working for the Gas Research Board, Imperial Chemical Industries. He worked for the Federated Foundries Ltd. in 1948, the John Brown Land Boilers Ltd. in 1954, and then returned to the G. & J. Weir Company. He returned to academia, after a successful career in industry, to become a professor of mechanical engineering at the Heriot-Watt University in Edinburgh and later to become the James Watt Chair at Glasgow University, from which he retired in 1979.

Immediately after the war, he turned his attention to the redesign of the ubiquitous coal-burning fireplaces, which were used in homes and offices all over the United Kingdom. His analysis of the heat balance of these fireplaces resulted in redesigns that saved tons of coal and helped reduce air pollution.

From 1956 to 1962, while working at the G. & J. Weir Company, he invented the Multistage Flash (MSF) Distillation System. This invention resulted from a careful analysis of the sources of entropy in various systems for water purification. Today the method of analysis he used is called "Second Law Analysis," but when he applied it to seawater demineralization, it was a novel idea. The first MSF plant was sold in Saudia Arabia, and Bob worked tirelessly to bring it on line, oftentimes at great risk to his health. It was dangerous to be inside the large flash chambers in the blazing Mideast sun. That plant established the commercial viability of the MSF process and its design was duplicated in many places. Multistage flash distillation represented an improvement in thermal efficiency of about two and one-half times. It also made practical the design of very large plants, upwards of millions of gallons per day of freshwater production. A one-million-gallon-per-day plant, based on the same principle, was built in San Diego as a demonstration plant by the U.S. Office of Saline Water, in the early 1950s. That plant was later dismantled and shipped to Guantanamo Bay, where it is still in use. It was always a source of bitterness for Bob Silver that because the G. & J. Weir Company failed to patent the design, many plants were built that did not have his care and attention, and, consequently, did not reach the efficiency and economy that was possible.

In 1962 he retired from the G. & J. Weir Company to become a professor of mechanical engineering at the Heriot-Watt University in Edinburgh. This was a difficult decision for him, as he had a great love for education and at the same time wanted to remain active in seawater demineralization. He wrote fundamental papers on the theory of condensation of pure liquids, on combustion, and on explosives.

In 1967 he returned to Glasgow University to become the James Watt Professor of Engineering. There he established a research program in seawater demineralization, to which students came from all over the world. Even after his retirement and passing, students still come to the center.

In 1971 he published a treatise on thermodynamics, developing the subject in a novel way, reflecting his many years of design experience.

He received many honors and awards, of which the following is a partial list:

- Foreign Associate of the National Academy of Engineering, 1979
- The George Stevenson Prize of the Institution of Mechanical Engineers for studies of convective circulation in water tube boilers, 1945
- The William Jack Prize from the University of Glasgow for the best D.Sc. thesis in the previous triennium, 1948
- The Heat Transfer Division Memorial Award of the American Society of Mechanical Engineers for his contributions to seawater demineralization, 1963
- The Commander of the Most Excellent Order of the British Empire, 1967
- The UNESCO Prize for Science for his work in desalination, 1968
- Honorary degree from Strathclyde University, 1984
- Honorary degree from the Robert Gordon University in Aberdeen, 1996.

Bob Silver had a great love of things Scottish. He was an avid fisherman and spent many hours on the Island of Mull, where he and his wife, Jean, had a summer home.

Bob was more than a physicist-engineer. He was passionate about the Scottish language and wrote many essays and poems in Scots. He wrote many essays on behalf of Scottish independence and stood in a parliamentary election as candidate for the Scottish National Party in the Glasgow Craigton constituency in 1979. His letters to the editor appeared in many issues of Scottish papers.

He was also a poet and playwright. His play *The Bruce* was published by the Saltire Society in 1986, read on BBC Radio, and produced at the Edinburgh Festival. A second edition of *The Bruce* was published in 1993 by the Scottish Cultural Press, incorporating two new scenes and other additions written for the Edinburgh Festival production of 1991. His play *The Picture* was staged in London and is still popular among many amateur companies.

A copy of his book *Conflict and Contexts*, published by Chapman, lies on my desk as I write. Among other things, it contains poems dedicated to his wife, Jean. They were married in 1937 and remained together for fifty-one years. I lift the first two and last two lines from this poem, dedicated to her after her death in 1989:

"Number Unobtainable"
Often my work kept us apart for weeks
We used the telephone to "keep in touch"

෨ඁ

From Curacao I talked to you in Mull
And touched you thus. I cannot touch you now.

My personal memory of Bob is that of a great conversationalist, whose wit and humor made each meeting too short. He could discourse intelligently on topics from theoretical physics and engineering to politics, economics, and religion. He was a stimulating and steadfast friend.

Bob is survived by his two sons, Colin and Alasdair, and his grandchildren Robbie and Catriona.

WERNER STUMM

1924–1999

BY JAMES J. MORGAN

Werner Stumm, professor emeritus at the Swiss Federal Institute of Technology (ETH Zürich) and former director of the Institute for Water Resources and Water Pollution Control (EAWAG) in Dübendorf, Switzerland, died at his home in Küsnacht, Switzerland, on April 14, 1999.

Werner Stumm was born in Wolfhalden, Switzerland, on October 8, 1924, and received his early education in Switzerland. He earned the Ph.D. in chemistry from the University of Zürich in 1952. His thesis research was in inorganic chemistry under the mentorship of Professor Gerold Schwarzenbach, a coordination chemist who was a pioneer in the use of complexing agents for chemical analysis. Werner's doctoral research centered on the use of ion-exchange resins and complexing agents for chemical analysis.

After receiving his Ph.D., Werner joined the chemistry staff of the Institute for Water Resources and Water Pollution Control, or EAWAG, a research institute of ETH Zürich. At EAWAG, he became interested for the first time in water treatment and water quality protection. Seeking to deepen his understanding of water chemistry, in 1954 and 1955 he spent a postdoctoral year at Harvard, in the Division of Engineering and Applied Physics, pursuing independent and unusually innovative research on iron corrosion in natural waters, which resulted in a highly original paper, "Calcium Carbonate Deposition at Iron Surfaces."

In 1956 he was called to Harvard as assistant professor of sanitary chemistry. At Harvard he initiated a research program into topics such as corrosion, rates of iron oxidation reactions in water, and coagulation of particles in water. In 1961 he became the Gordon McKay Associate Professor of Applied Chemistry, then Gordon McKay Professor of Applied Chemistry in 1964. He became a U.S. citizen in 1968.

From 1956 through 1970 Werner Stumm established a strong research and teaching program in water chemistry at Harvard. His laboratory became a magnet for doctoral students in environmental engineering, postdoctoral scholars in many disciplines, and visiting research scientists and engineers from the United States and other parts of the world. The emphasis in his research during the Harvard years was on application of fundamental chemistry to water quality engineering processes and ecosystem protection. Among the leading research accomplishments of that period in Werner Stumm's career were his work on rates of iron corrosion in relation to water chemistry, kinetic laws for iron and manganese oxidation in water, chemical aspects of coagulation processes in water, buffering in natural waters, the role and control of algal nutrients in water pollution, polymer flocculation of microorganisms, and chemical aspects of rapid filtration processes for particle removal. It is interesting to note that of the group of Ph.D. students and postdoctoral fellows who worked with Werner Stumm in the 1960s, five have since been elected to membership in National Academy of Engineering. His influence as a research leader and mentor was great indeed.

During his last few years as a professor at Harvard, Werner Stumm began to formulate a unified approach to natural water chemistry, a broad vision encompassing both applications to water technology and processes in the natural water environment. In 1966 he organized a symposium on "Equilibrium Concepts in Natural Waters" at a national meeting of the American Chemical Society. In the resulting proceedings, Werner first introduced the idea of aquatic chemistry as a unifying approach. Two traditions were joined: that of van't Hoff, Goldschmidt, and Sillén in explaining natural water compositions; and that of

Langelier, Buswell, Larson, and Black in improving corrosion control and water treatment. The widely used textbook *Aquatic Chemistry*, which first appeared in 1970, was one of the early fruits of his remarkable vision.

In 1970 Werner Stumm returned to Switzerland to become professor of aquatic chemistry at ETH and director of the EAWAG, the institute where he began his career eighteen years before. At the EAWAG Werner provided the intellectual leadership for a vigorous program of research in aquatic chemistry. At the same time that he guided the institute to a position at the forefront of environmental research, his own studies became more sharply focused on the chemistry of interfaces. Study of chemical processes in Swiss lakes and rivers received great emphasis. His own research had two principal goals: quantitative description of solid-water interface processes in natural waters; and understanding how to better protect aquatic systems under the stress of human activities. For protection of aquatic systems, Stumm urged an ecosystem perspective for all aquatic systems, integrating understanding of pertinent chemical, geochemical, biological and physical processes. Among the impacts on aquatic systems that EAWAG investigated under his leadership were those from atmospheric deposition, such as acid rain and fog, as well as a wide range of terrestrial inputs.

As EAWAG's director, Stumm shaped the institute along multidisciplinary lines in applied research, building up strength in both environmental sciences and environmental engineering. Through his efforts he helped bring EAWAG to a preeminent position worldwide. He recruited outstanding scientists and engineers to develop EAWAG's programs. Innovations in environmental analysis, water technology, modeling of aquatic systems, and chemical and biological dynamics in water were fostered during his time as the director. Scientists and engineers from the world over came to EAWAG to pursue research and to learn of new developments in environmental science and technology.

The fundamental contributions of Werner Stumm to understanding surface chemistry and particle removal in water technology earned him election to the National Academy of Engineering in 1991. The central theme of his research into particles and surfaces was that of chemical speciation, the distinct forms of charged and neutral chemical entities on particle surfaces. Surface species were in turn related to species concentrations in water through equilibrium, for example, protons, metal ions, anions, and polymers. In his early studies at Harvard, continuing on through his twenty-two years of research at EAWAG, the concept of *speciation* in water and on surfaces presented a satisfying picture of many key processes in environmental systems, such as adsorption of contaminants, rates of solid dissolution, oxidation-reduction processes in water, and surface catalysis. Werner Stumm played a seminal role in developing the surface complex formation model of adsorption to particles in water. The principal findings from Stumm's research were based primarily on macroscopic equilibrium and kinetic experiments, interpreted through simple chemical models, augmented by then-available tools for molecular observations, such as electron-nuclear double resonance and IR spectroscopy. Over the past decade, many of the important conclusions in his early work on surface speciation have been confirmed and extended by other scientists using newer spectroscopic and microscopic methods.

For Werner Stumm pursuit of a deep understanding of the processes governing natural water systems was a unifying theme of his life. He firmly believed that information at the molecular level was needed to understand local, regional, and global aspects of elemental cycles and impacts of pollution. Paralleling his love of natural water chemistry was his great dedication to teaching and mentoring young scientists and engineers. He was extremely generous of his time and energy. He was "Doctor Father" for more than forty Ph.D. students. During his career he authored or coauthored more than 300 research papers and produced sixteen books. In addition to his professorial tenures at Harvard and at ETH Zürich, he was, at various times in his career, visiting professor at the University of North Carolina, Chapel Hill; the University of Bern; University of Washington; Caltech; and Johns Hopkins. He traveled widely to many parts of the world to lecture on aquatic chemistry.

Werner was much honored in his lifetime. The University of Geneva, KTH Stockholm, University of Crete, Northwestern University, and Technion conferred honorary doctorates. He was recognized with the American Chemical Society's Monsanto Prize for Pollution Control in 1977, the Tyler Prize for Environmental Achievement in 1986, the Simon W. Freese Award of the American Society of Civil Engineers in 1991, the Goldschmidt Medal of the Geochemical Society in 1998, and the Stockholm Water Prize in 1999. On occasions of such honors, Werner unfailingly expressed his heartfelt appreciation to his students and scientific colleagues. On the occasion of receiving the Goldschmidt Medal he remarked: "It has been an especially gratifying privilege to be a teacher and to interact with my students over nearly five decades. My own research could not have been completed without the help and enthusiasm of [my] doctoral students." Werner Stumm was a man of great scientific and personal generosity. His contributions to the environment will be lasting. We cherish his legacy.

VICTOR G. SZEBEHELY

1921–1997

BY RICHARD H. BATTIN

VICTOR G. SZEBEHELY, professor of aerospace engineering and engineering mechanics at the University of Texas at Austin, died on September 13, 1997, at the age of seventy-six. Victor was admired and respected throughout the celestial mechanics and aerospace community. His contributions were both fundamental and extensive. His unassuming manner, which concealed a giant intellect, endeared him to all his colleagues and students.

Victor was born in Budapest, Hungary, in 1921. He managed to survive the Nazi occupation as a student and professor at the Technical University of Budapest. He received his M.S. degree in mechanical engineering in 1943 and his doctor of science degree in 1945 with a dissertation on the "three-body problem." (It would be almost twenty years before he would return to this most favored topic.) He was an assistant professor during the last years of the war, teaching mathematics and writing five books between 1944 and 1947: *Calculus for Engineers* (two volumes with two editions), *Exercise in Analysis* (two volumes), and *Graphical Methods in Applied Mathematics.* Then he immigrated to Canada—one of a generation of scientists who emigrated from Europe after World War II. (I don't remember Victor ever talking about life in Hungary in the war years, but he did keep in touch with many colleagues there throughout his life.)

Victor spent a year in Canada as a lecturer at McGill University in Montreal and then moved to the United States as a research assistant at Pennsylvania State University. In 1948 he went to the Virginia Polytechnic Institute and spent three years as an associate professor teaching fluid mechanics and dynamics.

Then began a six-year period from 1951 to 1957, during which he had three major responsibilities: lecturer at the University of Maryland, professorial lecturer at George Washington University, and manager of ship dynamics research at the David Taylor Model Basin. In 1954 he became a citizen of the United States. Two years later in 1956, a dimensionless number used in time-dependent unsteady flows was named "Szebehely's number," and in 1957 he was knighted by Queen Julianna of the Netherlands.

The year 1957 was also the year of the Russian *Sputnik* and the advent of the space age. Victor returned to his first love, orbital mechanics. He was appointed manager of space dynamics research at the General Electric Company Space Sciences Laboratory in Philadelphia, Pennsylvania. He also was a summer institute lecturer at Yale University. Then, in 1963, he went back to the academic world for good—first, as a visiting and then an associate professor at Yale University. He concentrated his teaching and research on celestial mechanics, with particular emphasis on the three-body problem and produced a wealth of contributions for which he will always be remembered.

His final move was to join the faculty of the University of Texas at Austin in 1968. He served as chairman of the Department of Aerospace Engineering and Engineering Mechanics from July 1977 to September 1981 and held the Richard B. Curran Centennial Chair of Engineering.

Victor was recognized for his many outstanding achievements by the American Astronautical Society (AAS) with the Dirk Brouwer Award in Celestial Mechanics and was named the first Brouwer Lecturer of the Dynamical Astronomy Division of the AAS at the 151st meeting of the Society in January 1978. Earlier in the September and October 1977 issues of the journal *Celestial Mechanics,* volume 16, an equation used to determine the gravitational potential of the earth, planets, satellites and galaxies was named "Szebehely's equation."

The proceedings of the Seventh International Conference on Mathematical Methods in Celestial Mechanics were dedicated to him on the occasion of his sixtieth birthday (1981). The next year he was elected to membership in the National Academy of Engineering, and in 1984 he was elected a fellow of the American Institute of Aeronautics and Astronautics.

An avalanche of honors followed: the Vanderlinden Award of the Belgian Royal Academy for scientific activities in 1987, and honorary doctor degree from Eötvös University of Budapest in 1991, election to membership in the European Academy in 1992, the Hocott Distinguished Centennial Engineering Award from the University of Texas in 1992, and the General Electric Senior Research Award from the American Society of Engineering Education in 1994.

Victor's major opus, *Theory of Orbits,* was published by the Academic Press in 1967 and reprinted in 1977. There was also a Russian translation by Duboshin and Romashov. It was an advanced reference text on the restricted problem of three bodies with theories and applications concerning periodic orbits, space trajectories, stability, and dynamical astronomy. His last book was pleasant, enjoyable, and eminently readable with the intriguing title *Adventures in Celestial Mechanics.* A second and expanded edition was published in 1998 by Hans Mark, a friend and colleague, the year after Victor passed away.

I first meet Victor when the Summer Institute of Dynamical Astronomy was held at the Massachusetts Institute of Technology in 1968 and 1969. He had a marvelously droll sense of humor and was a truly delightful person to know. My wife, Marge, and I enjoyed a pleasant evening with Victor at a lobster cookout on an island in Boston Harbor that summer in 1968. Later, when I told Victor that I was presenting a paper in Budapest at the 34th Congress of the International Astronautical Federation in October of 1983, he volunteered to write several of his Hungarian friends. Three of them contacted us during our stay in Budapest, and each gave us a private tour of his favorite haunts in and around the city. We remember fondly two wonderful evenings with Béla Balázs and his charming wife both in Budapest and in Vienna.

I recall with fondness a talk Victor gave during a plenary session at one of the astrodynamics conferences a few years ago. It concerned the chaos exhibited in the three-body problem that was a totally new phenomenon to me. I, together with the rest of the audience, was fascinated indeed. It was a pleasure to watch a real master make such a wonderful presentation.

I last saw Victor in Halifax, Nova Scotia, Canada, at an astrodynamics specialists meeting in August 1995. I learned of his death from one of my Massachusetts Institute of Technology students, who had done her undergraduate work with Victor the previous June at the University of Texas. It was sad news indeed.

Victor Szebehely was a wonderful friend, unpretentious, generous, and kind. It was a pleasure to know him, and he will be truly missed.

Hans J. P. von Ohain

HANS J. P. VON OHAIN

1911–1998

BY WILLIAM R. SEARS*

Hans Joachim Pabst von Ohain, inventor of the first turbo-jet aircraft engine that powered an aircraft, died on March 13, 1998. The first flight of his He S 3B engine was made in Marienehe, Germany, on August 27, 1939. After World War II he came to the United States as a "Paperclip" scientist to work in the Aerospace Research Laboratory (ARL) and the Air Force Aerospace Propulsion Laboratory (AFAPL). In both organizations he rose to the position of chief scientist. After retirement from the U.S. Air Force in 1979, he continued with independent developments. Von Ohain had the unique opportunity to observe the development of his original invention over almost sixty years, and to work in research on the many innovations for the turbojet engine for more than forty of those years. He is credited with fifty German patents and more than twenty U.S. patents.

Von Ohain was born into an aristocratic family that recognized early that their son's talent was in science rather than military service. He was educated at the prestigious Georg August University at Göttingen, completing the seven-year course of study for a doctorate in physics in only four years. His instructors included Ludwig Prandtl, Albert Betz, Walter Encke, Richard Courant, Robert Wichard Pohl, and Theodore von Kármán.

* Portions of this tribute were contributed by Margaret Connor, Historical Research Specialist, Universal Technology Corporation, Dayton, Ohio.

Göttingen University is considered to be the cradle of aerodynamic theory, and von Ohain was one of its most successful
students.

While von Ohain was completing his doctoral thesis on another subject, he made drawings of a design for a simple turbojet aircraft "device." With the help of a mechanic from the local
automotive repair shop, he built a model and applied for a
patent. His friend, Professor Pohl, recommended that he ob-
tain assistance when the project became too expensive. Twenty-
four-year-old von Ohain took his drawings to the head of one of
the largest aircraft manufacturers in Germany, Ernst Heinkel,
who immediately saw the possibilities in the new form of propulsion, and hired the young man.

Von Ohain's He S01 engine ran in March of 1937, fueled by
hydrogen. A month later, and totally unknown to each other,
Frank Whittle, in Britain, ran a turbojet powered by kerosene
and diesel liquid. Whittle's engine had an entirely different con-
figuration from von Ohain's and was based on his British patent
in 1930. By the summer of 1939, von Ohain improved his engine and installed the HE S 3B in the Heinkel-designed He-178
aircraft. The world-changing first flight of a turbojet-powered
aircraft on August 27, 1939, was overshadowed by Hitler's of-
fensive into Poland five days later, beginning World War II.

During the war, von Ohain developed other engines for
Heinkel with funding from the German Air Ministry, including
the He S 8 engine that powered the He 280, the world's first
turbojet-powered fighter aircraft, and the He S 011, considered
the world's most sophisticated jet engine in 1945. The war ended
before it powered a flight.

Von Ohain was among the German scientists selected to bring
their expertise to the United States following World War II. His
first assignment was in the Applied Research Section in engineering at what became Wright-Patterson Air Force Base near Dayton,
Ohio. It was quickly discovered that he had intellectual ability and
had unique experience in propulsion. He was chosen by Theodore
von Kármán and Frank Wattendorf to join them in planning an
advanced testing facility in Tullahoma, Tennessee, now known as
the Arnold Engineering Development Center.

Von Ohain worked in the research organization Aerospace (earlier, Aeronautical) Research Laboratory (ARL), which investigated a broad spectrum of disciplines useful for the U.S. Air Force. He distinguished himself with his thorough knowledge of technology. As one of his associates said, "He knew how nature worked!" Another said, "He was insightful and inciteful!" He was a mentor and inspiration to all, with a quiet and modest manner that could arrive at simple but effective solutions to difficult problems. His personal contributions were in the areas of direct energy conversion, including electrofluid-dynamic energy conversion (EFD), magnetohydro-dynamics (MHD), and magnetofluid-dynamics (MFD); the colloid gas core reactor; thrust augmentation, including V/STOL research and the "jet wing"; and advanced supersonic flow machinery. He acted as consultant for other organizations and as mentor for students at the Air Force Institute of Technology. In 1963 he became chief scientist of the ARL, responsible to be adviser for all the work of the laboratory. In 1966 he and Sir Frank Whittle shared the American Institute of Aeronautics and Astronautics Goddard Award "for brilliant discovery and outstanding contributions over a period of time in the engineering science of energy conversion," and became friends. They enjoyed discussing their solutions to problems with the early engines.

In 1975 the ARL was disbanded. Von Ohain left basic research to return to his first love, propulsion, and became chief scientist for the AFAPL, working closely with another propulsion legend, Cliff Simpson. His technical contributions to the Air Force and in international circles drew attention to his earlier achievements. Many honors and awards came to him from the Air Force and from professional associations. An interesting meeting was held in Dayton in 1978, an encounter between the jet engine inventors, where von Ohain and Whittle discussed their inventions before an open session at the Air Force Museum.

Von Ohain retired from his Air Force job in 1979. He continued professional contributions at the University of Dayton Research Institute, taught classes at the University of Dayton and the University of Florida at Gainesville, led seminars at the Air Force Academy and in Taiwan, and continued to receive presti-

gious national and international awards. He was the Charles
Lindbergh Professor at the National Air and Space Museum of
the Smithsonian Institution in 1985. In 1991 the Charles Stark
Draper Prize and gold medal, the "Nobel Prize" of engineering,
was awarded jointly to Hans von Ohain and Sir Frank Whittle.
He received the Daniel Guggenheim Medal from the American
Society of Mechanical Engineers/Society of Automotive Engi-
neers/American Institute of Aeronautics and Astronautics, and
the Rudolf Diesel Award and the Prandtl Ring from Germany.
Von Ohain is enshrined in the Deutsches Museum in Munich,
the National Aviation Hall of Fame, the International Aerospace
Hall of Fame in San Diego, and the Engineering and Science
Hall of Fame in Dayton.

Von Ohain met the woman he married, Hanny Schukat, in
1947 at a Christmas dinner her parents had for some of the
Paperclip scientists. He and Hanny had four children, Stephen,
Christopher, Katherine, and Stephanie. Von Ohain, who was a
bachelor until age thirty-seven, enjoyed family life.

Hans von Ohain is remembered by his associates and friends
for more than his technical achievements. He had warmth, humor, and kindness, and was always looking to the next possibility, to the future. His life was summed up by his friend, General
Philippe Bouchard, at a memorial service; "This patient, humble,
gentle, creative, family-oriented person just happened to have
invented the jet engine."

ELMER P. WHEATON

1909–1997

BY JAMES G. WENZEL

Elmer P. Wheaton, a director and associate of Marine Development Associates, Inc. and former vice-president/general manager of the Research and Development Division, Lockheed Missiles and Space Company, and corporate vice-president of engineering, Douglas Aircraft Corporation, died at Stanford Hospital on December 28, 1997, at the age of eighty-eight. Elmer Wheaton was a trail-blazing engineer who lived in Portola Valley, California, for over thirty-five years, a beautiful estate area supporting Silicon Valley. A review of Elmer's early days shows a man willing to start at the bottom, to be innovative, and work his way to the top.

Elmer Wheaton was born in Elyria, Ohio, on August 15, 1909, the son of Harry and Lizzie Nicholl Wheaton. The family moved to Los Angeles in 1912, where two younger brothers were born, Bill and Harry, and, where Elmer launched his technical and engineering career.

Although during his childhood he was ill much of the time, and the family was wealthy, he wanted to earn his own money. His first job was delivering newspapers, until he was confined to his home and moved to a special remedial class due to his absence. At age eleven and studying *Boy's Life*, he built a crystal radio receiver from parts and set up a radio room and a telephone pole antenna. Later he built a vacuum tube receiver using a UVI

241

99 tube with a varometer and a variable condenser. With it he could pick up stations all over the United States as well as intercept radio telephone calls from Catalina Island.

During high school, Elmer's favorite subject was physics. Stimulated by a wonderful teacher, he would stay after school, running his own experiments of interest. On high school graduation in 1929, he won a prize for an essay entitled "The Commercial Possibilities of Aviation." The paper reviewed the history of aviation, the technologies required, the present status, and the future potential—an accurate prediction and the direction of Elmer's early career.

As a result of his high school experiences, Elmer obtained his higher education at Pomona College, majoring in physics. In addition to aviation, he became intrigued with the oceans, attending summer school at Pomona's Marine Laboratory in Laguna Beach. His physics work also became more exciting as he helped build one of the first television receivers and transmitters, using photocells he made and whirling disks for scanning. He received some wonderful guidance from his professor, Dr. Teleston. "You are able to look at the forest and not get blocked by the underbrush. Do not try to be a detail man, but one who understands the whole picture!" This sound advice became the guide for much of Elmer Wheaton's technical and engineering management career.

His physics research became even more exciting with part-time work at Caltech in furthering the development of coating nonmetallic surfaces with thin films of metal by evaporation or sputtering. The goals of this work were to make electronic fibers for gas discharge experiments and to use them in "silvering" mirrors with thin films of metal. One of the first aluminum-coated mirrors was built using this process. Wheaton graduated from Pomona College in 1933 with a B.A. degree in physics and a sound technical foundation for managing research and development activities.

However, tough years were ahead for Elmer Wheaton. It was in the middle of the depression and jobs were scarce. His physics professor, Dr. Teleston, came to his rescue and set him up for his first real job, serving as a strikebreaker for Columbia in the motion picture industry. The job involved working on sound track recordings and the associated filter networks to permit correction of the problems in recording voices of certain silent screen stars. All of Elmer's physics background, including his work on electrometer fibers was involved. He also now thought he had the financial basis for starting a home and married his beautiful and beloved life partner, Martha, in October 1933.

Life for the happy young couple became difficult. With the Christmas holiday shutdown, the job at Columbia Pictures disappeared, and survival meant doing everything from wiring lamps on cooking ranges to unloading freight cars. But his career got back on track through one of his many friends, by hiring into Douglas Aircraft in 1934, installing soundproofing in the DC-2 at $0.45 an hour. Subsequent tasks in the installation and riveting of subassemblies taught him another lesson vital to project engineering—the many structural interference problems requiring engineering solutions. A tour in production control gave further evidence of these issues and education in interference management. Elmer's dedication to hard work and understanding the big picture finally resulted in a transfer into engineering in 1935, and a project clerk task in the DC-2 Project Office. At last Elmer had a job he believed had a long-term technical future.

Elmer's interests in the oceans, physics, and engineering, and the need for extra income, caused him to develop a new commercial diving helmet called "The Nautilus." The system consisted of the helmet, weights, a topside pump, fifty feet of hose, and a sturdy carrying case. Tests at Laguna Beach were highly successful with much publicity on potential ocean exploration. However, due to the depression, commercialization timing was not right. Only two units were sold, and the exciting pioneering venture was terminated.

After only a few months in the engineering department at Douglas, Elmer had the opportunity to play a lead role in developing a new technology then in its infancy—acoustic quieting of commercial transport aircraft. Because of his background in applied acoustics at Columbia Pictures, he was assigned to work with Henry Bruderlin from the Chief Engineers Office. As a team they tackled the sound control problems of the Douglas DST (DC-3). This task was soon expanded to include the overall problem of vibration control and flutter. Pioneering in the application of electrical test instrumentation and with his background in physics, Elmer broadened his involvement into other fields of technology. He began joint projects with the Douglas Research Group and set the foundation for his career as an aerospace engineering, research, and development executive. It is also interesting to note that, as a young aspiring engineer, Elmer earned $101.58 in the month of March 1936. It was truly a different world!

With the start of World War II, there was a major expansion within the aircraft industry, with new divisions being formed within Douglas, and the departure of a few senior executives to start their own companies. The growing interest in missiles and his demonstrated advanced research and development capability vaulted Elmer into the role of chief missiles project engineer at Douglas in 1945. His full responsibility for all missile development included the Nike Ajax, Nike Hercules (antiaircraft), Sparrow I, II, and III (air-to-air), Genie, Corporal E, and Honest John (ground-to-ground). In 1955 with the development of the Thor intermediate-range ballistic missile, a new division was formed, and Elmer Wheaton became vice-president of engineering, missiles and space systems in 1958. Three years later, in 1961, he reached the top engineering position at Douglas Aircraft Corporation, the corporate vice-president, engineering.

With the development of Polaris and a major corporate thrust into space systems, Lockheed formed its Missile & Space Company (LMSC) in Sunnyvale, California. Elmer Wheaton resigned from Douglas in 1962 and became vice-president, research and development, LMSC, and a Lockheed corporate vice-president. The LMSC president, L. Eugene Root, launched "Project Enterprise," aimed at diversifying aerospace technology into other applicable fields, and based on proposals and recommendations from the companies engineers. One of the finest research laboratories in aerospace had already been formed at LMSC to support all mainline programs and assigned to Wheaton. It was logical that all advanced research and development also be put under Elmer Wheaton for nurturing and development. For diversification, he fully subscribed to the philosophy of Lockheed's founder, Bob Gross, who said, "look far ahead, where the horizons are absolutely unlimited!" Elmer had an innovative mind, was a very good listener, saw the "big picture" and trusted his key people—keys to inspiration and program success, and a direct example of the early observation of Dr. Teleston at Pomona College. The results reflected that approach, with the formation of a "greenhouse" of highly successful programs in ground vehicles, ocean systems, airborne systems, information systems, and nuclear test services.

My long and productive personal relationship with Elmer resulted from my Project Enterprise proposal to develop ocean systems, a direct application of aerospace technology and a major opportunity for the corporation. In my role as vice-president of ocean systems, it was indeed a privilege to work for Elmer and to know you could bank on his support. However, as supportive as Elmer was, he was also tough. He knew and loved the oceans. One morning he told me, "Jim, if you are ever going to build successful ocean hardware, you need to personally understand the environment in which it has to operate. I want you to learn how to scuba dive!" I complained, "but Elmer, I understand oceanography, and I suffer from claustrophobia. I cannot even dive to the deep end of my swimming pool without my ears killing me!" Wheaton's response—"We will teach you!"—a subtle order. He was right and we spent twenty-five years diving together in an organization called Sea-Space Symposium, a group of ocean and aerospace executives sharing technologies, advice, and counsel. I became acquainted with a whole new environment and gained respect for the sea.

Ocean engineering was close to his heart and he strongly supported our thrusts into deep-diving submersibles, the Deep Quest research submarine, development of the navy's Submarine Rescue System (DSRV), and the technology for 20,000-foot operations. Commercial applications of this technology included offshore oil, deep-ocean recovery, ocean mining, and ocean energy.

Mr. Wheaton's professional contributions to research and engineering were recognized far outside Douglas and Lockheed.

He served as a member of the Special Industry Committee on Missiles, Office of the Assistant Secretary of the Air Force, Research and Development, and chairman of the Guided Missile Council-Aerospace Industries Association. He was appointed to the first National Committee of Ocean and Atmosphere in 1973, recommended formation of the National Oceanic and Atmospheric Administration, and served as president of the Engineering Committee for Ocean Research, a United Nations Advisory Committee. Elmer also served as a member of President Nixon's Task Force on Oceanography. He received many awards, including certificates of merit for outstanding contributions from the Office of Scientific Research and Development and the war and navy departments, the Robert M. Thompson Award for Outstanding Civilian Leadership from the Navy League of the United States, the Aerospace Contribution to Society Award from the American Institute of Aeronautics and Astronautics, and the Distinguished Service Award from the Institute of Electrical and Electronics Engineers Oceanic Engineering Society. Elmer Wheaton's most treasured award was his election to the National Academy of Engineering in 1967 as one of the earliest aerospace industry executives so honored.

Elmer Wheaton retired from Lockheed in 1974 but continued his technical and advisory involvement as a consultant. With his interests in the oceans, he joined Marine Development Associates, Inc., as both an associate and director, where he provided encouragement, active support, and counsel until his death.

Elmer Wheaton was not only an innovative engineer but also a trail-blazing equestrian. He was a member of the San Mateo County Mounted Patrol and the Shack Riders. Upon retirement, he took on the job of rebuilding trails as a member of the San Mateo Trail Committee, and worked to extend trails into the Portola Valley and for the Woodside Trail Club. As he dealt with his subordinates, so he dealt with his horse—considering the horse's well-being first, and his own second.

Elmer Wheaton was also deeply spiritual, serving as an active member of Christ Episcopal Church in Portola Valley. His spiritual convictions were the foundation for his life. Elmer is survived by his lovely wife, Martha, two children—Markley Wheaton and Sara Perry—two grandchildren, and one great-grandson.

Elmer P. Wheaton was truly an inspirational leader in aerospace research and engineering, an industry giant, a pioneer in his field, and a wonderful and faithful friend. He is greatly respected and missed by all who knew and worked with him.

E C Whitney

EUGENE C. WHITNEY

1913–1998

BY EDWIN L. HARDER AND LEE A. KILGORE

T HE CENTENNIAL CELEBRATION of the Institute of Electrical and Electronics Engineers in 1984 revealed much about the pioneers of electrical engineering. It revealed that when Benjamin Lamme designed the electrical machines for Niagara Falls, they were four times larger than any electrical machines that had ever been built. When Edwin Harder mentioned this to Gene Whitney, he said, "Yes, that's right—until I built the Grand Coulee machines. They were six times larger than the largest previous machines." The parts had to be shipped out to Grand Coulee and assembled in the power plant. Then they were simply started, and they have worked perfectly since.

Because electrical machines six times the size of those at Grand Coulee are not likely to be needed in the world, Whitney's record is likely to stand, and by this measure he remains the greatest hydro machine designer in the world!

In a chance meeting years later with Whitney's boss at the time of Grand Coulee, he was still amazed that Gene had been able to design those tremendous machines and that they had worked perfectly from the start.

Whitney designed hydro machines for dams and pumped storage projects all over the United States. He was the consultant for the huge Itapu project in Brazil. He designed the electrical machines for Muddy Run, a pumped storage project on the lower Susquehanna River. He was present when the machines were first to be started. The operator was reluctant to take the first step. Gene said, "Call your boss." The boss said, "If Gene says to start the machines, start them." So they did, and water rose from the lower Susquehanna River to the upper reservoir, 400 feet above, on the Piedmont Plateau, through which the Susquehanna River had cut its valley. Thereafter the upper reservoir was refilled every weekend and drawn down day by day throughout the week (partially refilled at night), to provide peaking power for the Philadelphia Electric system.

Whitney's career was with the Westinghouse Electric Company. He arrived just in time to help clean up after the 1936 flood. Starting as a design engineer, he became manager of engineering for large motors and water-wheel generators. He developed many concepts and patents for winding, steel damper bars, brushless exciters, and efficiency and cost reductions.

Gene's romance with Jina (Nina-Jean) Knudson started in high school and continued in college at Flint Junior College and the University of Michigan. They were married in Pittsburgh, after Gene had joined Westinghouse, on August 1, 1937.

They had three children, Margaret (Lessman), James, and Alan. Gene and Jina both enjoyed outdoor activities, including camping, canoeing, swimming, and tennis. They were members of the Sylvan Canoe Club on the Allegheny River in Pittsburgh and shared in club activities with their many friends. Gene was a pillar of his church and took an active part in it.

Gene was the recipient of many honors. He received the Westinghouse Order of Merit in 1964, the Institute of Electrical and Electronics Engineers (IEEE) Nikola Tesla Award in 1985, and was an IEEE fellow. He was elected to the National Academy of Engineering in 1986.

After retirement Gene did consulting work for hydro projects all over the world. He was active in the Boy Scouts, the Kiwanis Club, and in many family activities. He was loved and admired by all his friends.

FRANK WHITTLE

1907–1996

BY RICHARD J. COAR

ONE OF THE twentieth century's best "hands on" engineers, Sir Frank Whittle, will be remembered as the earliest inventor of the aircraft turbojet engine, and for his persistence in demonstrating its feasibility in the face of initial rejection and despite later bureaucratic roadblocks thrown in his path by the British government. During the latter half of the 20th century, billions of dollars have been invested by governments and by engine manufacturers to develop Whittle's invention into remarkable propulsion systems that have changed the face of the world. Now no point on the globe is more than a day away by air; aircraft fly routinely faster than Mach 3, at more than 70,000 feet of altitude; and 400 passengers can be carried nonstop across the country using less petroleum than if they traveled by car or train.

Whittle was born of working-class parents in Coventry, England, on June 1, 1907, and attended local schools until age fifteen. Then he tried to join the Royal Air Force as an aircraft apprentice but flunked the physical exam for being undersize. Now early in his career, we see Whittle's persistence paying off— less than a year later, by diet and exercise, he had added three inches to his height and three inches to his chest measurement to enter the September 1923 class of the Royal Air Force. During Whittle's three years there, he was trained as a metal aircraft rigger. Probably because of the aircraft engineering aptitude he displayed building a large powered model aircraft in off-duty hours at the Model Aircraft Society, Whittle was one of five from his 600-man apprentice class selected for flight cadet training at the R.A.F. College, Cranwell. In his two years at Cranwell, Whittle learned to fly (surviving an engine failure in flight and the total loss of an airplane he flew into a tree on a foggy go-around), and he began thinking about how to achieve high-speed, long-range, high-altitude flight. His thesis was the starting point for his subsequent work on jet propulsion: "Future Developments in Aircraft Design." His flying instructor's final comments in Whittle's flight log included these words in red ink "inclined to perform to gallery and flies too low." Frank loved aerobatics.

While qualifying to be a flight instructor at the Central Flying School in 1929, Whittle had his first thought of using a turbine to produce a propelling jet instead of turning a propeller. The school's commandant brought this invention to the attention of the Air Ministry, who then requested Whittle to report there with his sketches and calculations. As Whittle put it later, "The result was depressing," and he returned in low spirits. He had met the not-invented-here syndrome head-on. Before the year was over, the Air Ministry informed him that because his scheme was a "form of gas turbine, it was considered to be impractical, as materials did not then exist capable of withstanding the combination of high temperatures and high stresses that would be necessary." It seems likely that the ministry really believed that such materials would soon enough become available, because it was already funding a program at its own laboratory under Dr. A. A. Griffith to develop a turbine to drive a propeller.

At the flying school, one of his instructors offered to help Whittle apply for a patent, and this application was filed on January 16, 1930. The Air Ministry advised Whittle that it had no official interest in the patent, so it was not put on the Secret list, and it was published worldwide in its 1932 issue. (Unfortunately, Whittle allowed the patent to lapse in 1935 when he decided not to spend the money for a renewal fee. None of us is perfect.) As a qualified flying instructor and then test pilot, Whittle managed to crash a few more airplanes and learned the flying peculiarities of eighteen different kinds of aircraft. A nonswimmer, he was fortunate to escape with his life during a year and a half of being catapulted from new experimental catapults. To get backing for his jet engine during this period, Whittle made overtures to four commercial firms, but without results.

When it came time, after four years with a permanent commission, to select a specialist course of advanced training, Whittle chose engineering. In August 1932 he was posted to the officers' engineering course at Henlow, where he completed the twenty-four-month course in eighteen months. The Air Ministry had by then discontinued its practice of sending one or two officers from Henlow on to Cambridge University for the Mechanical Sciences Tripos (an honors course named after the three-legged stool one sat on to take the oral examination). Whittle persisted again and got the ministry to make an exception, so in July 1934 after being promoted to flight lieutenant, he was attached to the Cambridge University Air Squadron. In two years instead of the usual three, he took first-class honors and was then well grounded in the aerodynamic and material sciences he would need to succeed with his jet engine invention.

Whittle recognized the important contribution made to his jet engine by two ex-RAF officers, Dudley Williams and J. C. B. Tinling, who approached Whittle at Cambridge and convinced him they could find investors to sponsor development of the jet engine. The outcome of these discussions was a "Four Party Agreement" sanctioned by the Air Ministry, between Whittle, Williams, Tinling, and the investment firm Falk & Partners, and the incorporation in March 1936 of Power Jets, Limited. Because Whittle was a serving officer in the Royal Air Force, Power Jet's field of play was severely circumscribed by the Air Ministry—25 percent of Whittle's interest in the venture was allotted to the Crown; he was entitled to act as honorary chief engineer, but only off-duty and no more than six hours per week; all of Whittle's patent rights were assigned to the company, but the government retained right of "Free Crown Use." With very little capital, no employees, no facilities, and an unproved concept, one must be amazed that Whittle accomplished what he did, and not be surprised that his health failed in the end.

Power Jets placed orders with the B.T-H (British Thompson-Houston) Company to provide design drawings of an experimental engine based on requirements Whittle had laid down at Cambridge to manufacture parts, and to make facilities available for testing, all on a cost-plus basis. B.T-H had been selected because it had experience supplying industrial turbines and compressors. It soon became clear that this background was not relevant to aircraft engines. Whittle rejected B.T-H's first design and then gave B.T-H a preliminary design to use. Despite many procurement difficulties, and the fact that neither the turbine nor the compressor had been run as an individual component, the first run of the engine was self-sustaining on March 12, 1937.

The next two years were fraught with difficulties on every front—Falk failed to find adequate funds; the Air Ministry threatened to terminate Whittle's special duty assignment because progress was so slow; B.T-H evicted Power Jets from the marginal facilities they were using but provided space in an abandoned foundry; and every engine test disclosed some new mechanical or aerodynamic problem. A visitor to Whittle's dilapidated office in the foundry at that time might find him with his rifle pointed out the window shooting rabbits. Whittle had assumed that B.H-T, whose primary business was turbines, at least knew how to design them, but the tests showed the jet's turbine efficiency to be low. Whittle, still a graduate student, gave B.T-H new aerodynamics that solved the problem. The fact that the boy aerodynamicist knew more about turbines than the old pros soured the relationship from that point forward. Over this two-year period, enough funds were slowly provided by the Air Ministry so that on June 30, 1939, Power Jets demonstrated to the ministry's director of scientific research a twenty-minute engine run up to 94 percent of design speed. This one demonstration led the director to conclude they now had the basis for an aero-engine. The ministry agreed to pick up the costs of parts for the experimental engine and gave Power Jets a contract for a flight test engine that was subcontracted to B.T-H. The ministry also contracted with Gloster Aircraft for an experimental aircraft, the E.28/29. When war broke out, the Air Ministry had already decided to pursue Whittle's turbojet work and to continue Whittle's appointment to Power Jets.

The W.1 experimental flight test engine powered the first

British jet flight successfully on May 15, 1941. By the end of 1940, before the E.28/29 had flown, the Air Ministry decided to have the W.2, a higher thrust engine, developed and produced to power a twin-engine jet fighter, the F9/40 *Meteor*. The ministry named the Rover Company to produce the engine, a choice that soon proved disastrous. Rover decided to design its own engine rather than use Whittle's design. Rover had no background in aircraft engine development or manufacture and refused to take Whittle's technical advice to correct the engine's problems. By December 1942 the production program was so far behind schedule that the new ministry of aircraft production transferred the production program to Rolls Royce. Then with close cooperation the mode between Rolls and Whittle's team, and with Rolls' aggressive technical policy, the 100-hour type test of the W.2 was completed only five months later. Whittle's special-duty-list attachment to Power Jets continued until 1946, with responsibility for the design of the W.2b (the Rolls Royce "Welland"), the W.2/500, and W.2/700 ('Parents' of the Rolls Royce Derwent and Nene).

In Germany at Ernst Heinkel's factory, Hans von Ohain had begun experiments in secret and had bench-tested his jet engine in 1937. This He S 3B engine powered the world's first turbojet aircraft flight on August 27, 1939. Although this reduction to practice preceded the British flight, Whittle is usually considered to be the earlier inventor. In any event, both British and German governments failed to exploit the turbojet engine aggressively, so this new invention was not a factor in the conduct of World War II. The few Me 262s (powered by two Jumo 004 axial compressor turbojets) flown by the Germans at the end of the war were 100 miles per hour faster than Allied fighters, and on one occasion in 1944 destroyed thirty-two B-17 bombers out of a flight of thirty-six. Fortunately the Me 262s were unreliable, too few, and too late—Allied bombing had left the Nazis little fuel for flying.

In October 1941, the U.S. Army Air Corps delivered a W.lx engine, the W.2b drawings, and a team of three from Power Jets Ltd. to the General Electric Company. This was the beginning of turbojet development in the United States. Tradition says

General Electric was selected for turbojet development because the company had relevant turbosupercharger experience, and because the administration wanted no interference with the aircraft engine production needed to meet Roosevelt's May 1940 call for 50,000 planes a year. Some say General H.H. "Hap" Arnold had another concern—that if he gave the job to a traditional engine manufacturer, it might suffer fatally from the not-invented-here syndrome.

In 1944 Power Jets was nationalized and in April 1946 merged with the aircraft gas turbine section of the Royal Aircraft Establishment to form the National Gas Turbine Establishment, whose sole function was limited to conducting research and to assisting the aircraft industry. In Whittle's words, the company he had cofounded and nurtured "was smothered to death by the government." This ended Whittle's activities in the design and development of engines. After resigning from Power Jets, he was appointed adviser to the Ministry of Supply and retired in 1948 with the rank of air commodore. He was knighted by King George VI, and finally in May 1948 he was awarded 100,000 pounds on the recommendation of the Royal Commission on Rewards to Inventors.

Sir Frank remained active in retirement, consulting, lecturing, and writing his book *Jet—The Story of a Pioneer*. Separated from his first wife since 1952, he was divorced in 1976 and emigrated to the United States, where he married Hazel Hall. At age seventy, Frank Whittle would still confound younger engineers, who were apt to solve their aerodynamics problems on multimillion-dollar computers, by quickly getting useful results on the back of an envelope using his 5-inch slide rule. He closed his colorful career in the position of research professor at the U.S. Naval Academy. His textbook on gas turbine aerodynamics was published in 1981.

In addition to his knighthood, Whittle's work has been recognized by awards and medals from eight different countries, by eleven honorary doctorates, and by honorary membership in more than twenty professional or learned societies. He was elected by his peers a foreign associate of the National Academy of Engineering in 1979, and in 1991 shared with Hans von Ohain the Academy's Charles Stark Draper Prize of $375,000.

F. Karl Willenbrock

F. KARL WILLENBROCK

1920–1995

BY JOHN G. TRUXAL

F. KARL WILLENBROCK, retired leader of engineering programs in both academia and government, died August 24, 1995, in Alexandria, Virginia.

Karl was born in New York City and started his engineering career with the bachelor's of science degree with highest honors at Brown University. He completed his formal education with the master's and doctoral degrees in applied physics from Harvard University.

Karl remained at Harvard until 1967 as a research fellow, lecturer, laboratory director, and associate dean. During this period, he took responsibility for running the undergraduate and graduate engineering programs, while at the same time he was deeply involved in teaching.

In 1967 Karl moved for three years to the position of provost and professor of engineering and applied science at the State University of New York at Buffalo. Here, as one of the two leaders of engineering programs in SUNY, he brought a vision of the role of engineering at a public university—the important relations with statewide industry to complement the academic programs and the critical coordination of SUNY degree programs with the two-year colleges and the secondary schools. In addition, he led the expansion of the Buffalo program in the emerging information sciences.

Karl's next position was as director of the Institute of Applied Technology at the National Bureau of Standards (NBS). Here he directed the NBS work in several critical areas at a time when engineering was just beginning its concern with sociotechnical problems.

This work included fire prevention and research, the applications of operations research to urban and municipal problems, and the development of basic specifications for manufacturing techniques in electronics.

These activities contributed to the evolution of a proactive role in the National Bureau of Standards and, more broadly, the Department of Commerce. Well after Karl's departure, the NBS name was changed to the National Institute of Standards and Technology (NIST), and the agency mission was broadened to encompass many of the ideas that Karl first envisioned.

Karl continued the unusual combination of academic and government service with his 1976 move to the position of dean of engineering and Cecil and Ida Green Professor of Engineering at Southern Methodist University, where again the academic programs were closely allied with the work of regional industry.

In 1986 Karl left the university for a three-year stint as executive director of the American Society for Engineering Education, where he brought his vision of the central role of engineering education in the evolving information revolution in industry. This leadership role continued until his retirement with two years as National Science Foundation assistant director for scientific, technological, and international affairs, senior scientist in the Technology Administration at the Department of Commerce, and visiting professor of engineering and public policy at Carnegie Mellon University.

Throughout his career, Karl served frequently as a consultant to industrial and governmental organizations. He was a leader, as well, in professional societies—for example, as president of the Institute of Electrical and Electronics Engineers. He had a variety of committee responsibilities at the National Academy of Engineering, including membership on the Council of the NAE from 1980 to 1986.

For those of us who were among his many friends and admirers, Karl was always on the lookout for new directions in which the engineer's approach and analysis opened the doors. His total commitment to his work led to his unwavering enthusiasm for new ideas. It was not unusual to receive a phone call from Karl on an early Sunday evening when he had thought of a novel way in which engineering might contribute to human welfare.

CHIA–SHUN YIH

1918–1997

BY YUAN–CHENG FUNG

CHIA-SHUN YIH was a humane, humorous, and poetic fluid dynamicist. He invented elegant mathematical transformations that simplify the differential equations and boundary conditions of the flow of nonhomogeneous fluids. He devised efficient methods of calculations. He discovered many exact or closed form solutions of waves and instabilities in fluid flow, and of course also many approximate solutions. He devised efficient calculations and pertinent experiments. He developed the field of stratified flow for its beauty and applications to atmospheric, oceanic, and other flows of scientific, environmental, and industrial interest. In his memory, his friends organized an international symposium at the U.S. National Congress of Applied Mechanics in June 1998, and dedicated a book, *Fluid Dynamics at the Interfaces* (Cambridge University Press, 1999), to him.

Chia-Shun Yih was born on July 25, 1918, in Kweiyang City, Kweizhou Province, which lies in the southern midwest part of China. Kweizhou is a beautiful mountainous country. Chia-Shun was born into a scholarly family, the son of Yih Ding-Jan and Hsiao Wan-Lan. His father was a specialist on silk and silkworm culture. His father's profession was fortunate for me, because it made his father come to work in Kiangsu Province, which lies on the east coast of China, where I was born, where every family raised silkworms in the spring. Chia-Shun attended junior middle school (grades 7 to 9) in Zhengkiang, the provincial capital of

Kiangsu. Then he and I both passed the entrance exam of the Soozhou Senior Middle School (grades 10 to 12) and entered in 1934. Soozhou has a long history. It was the capital of the Kingdom of Woo (585 B.C. to 490 B.C.). Our school ground was old and beautiful. The oldest hall of the school, where we often took examinations, was called the Purple Sun Hall, in honor of Master Zhu Hsi (1130 to 1200 AD). The walls of the hall were lined with plaques of black stone on which Zhu Hsi's poems and lectures were carved. The halo of tradition was real.

While we were in high school, the storm of war was gathering in China. Japan had occupied Manchuria in 1931 and invaded Shanghai in 1932. Full-scale war between China and Japan finally broke out on July 7, 1937, soon after our graduation from high school. We managed to take the entrance examination of the National Central University and got accepted. The university was located originally in Nanjing, the capital of China at that time. Before we could enter, however, it was moved to Chongqing, in Sichuan Province in the central midwest of China.

At our university, Chia-Shun studied, among other things, mathematics and the theory and design of bridges. Our college years were spent in makeshift classrooms and laboratories, classes at the crack of dawn to avoid air raids, long hours in the dugouts, military training, and an endless stream of exciting or sad news. One wintry day, Japanese planes came and bombed out our simple shower hut, and for weeks afterward some of us had to bathe in the emerald water of the nearby Chia-Ling River, beautiful but cold.

After graduation, Chia-Shun worked first in the National Hydraulics Laboratory in Guanshien, Sichuan. There he studied the work of Li Bing, who more than 2,300 years ago, invented a system of constructing and reconstructing control dikes every year, which works to this day. Li Bing's design made Chengdu plain one of the richest areas in China for 2,300 years. Then Chia-Shun worked for the Chinese Bridge Company in Kweiyang, his hometown, designing highway bridges. In 1944 he taught at Kweizhou University. Then he married Loh Hung-Kwei, who gave birth to their first son, Yiu Yo Yih. The marriage lasted only a few years.

Then a group of American professors visited China and upon their return raised forty-some graduate scholarships from various American universities and offered them to the Chinese Ministry of Education. By nationwide examinations, the Ministry of Education chose forty-two students to study in the United States. We were among the forty-two, and in 1945 we came to the United States via India.

After a brief stay at Purdue University, Chia-Shun went to the University of Iowa to study fluid mechanics with Hunter Rouse and John McNown, with whom he maintained a warm friendship throughout his life. He signed up also for courses in music appreciation and French conversation. The young instructor of French conversation was Shirley Ashman from Maine. Chia-Shun and Shirley fell in love and were married in 1949.

In the summer of 1947, Chia-Shun went to Brown University and listened to C.C. Lin's lectures on fluid dynamics and was inspired. On returning to Iowa, he told me that he was concentrating his study on the smoke from a lighted cigarette. The smoke rises, curls up, becomes turbulent, and disperses. He was fascinated. His mentor, Hunter Rouse, encouraged him to pursue the subject in depth. It became a part of his Ph.D. dissertation. From that little seed a whole field grew up in his mind. In the following years, Chia-Shun developed the general theory of the dynamics of nonhomogeneous fluid with broad applications. This beginning of a big endeavor with a small subject is a trait of his research career, consistent with his love of poetry. A poet sees the arrival of spring in a single flower bud. The cigarette smoke contains the same truth and same beauty as the larger subjects.

Chia-Shun got his Ph.D. in 1948. From 1948 to 1955, Chia-Shun taught and conducted research at the University of Wisconsin, the University of British Columbia, Colorado A&M University, the University of Nancy in France, and the University of Iowa. He finally settled down at the University of Michigan in Ann Arbor. For sabbatical leave he went to Europe. He spent a year (1959 to 1960) at Cambridge University, England, a year (1964) in Geneva, another year (1970 to 1971) in the Universities of Paris and Grenoble in France, and a year (1977 to 1978) at Chatoux Lab in Paris and the Technische Hochschule Karlsruhe, in Germany. After he retired in 1988, he served as a graduate research professor at the University of Florida in Gainesville for three years.

Honors followed Chia-Shun's achievements. In 1968 the University of Michigan celebrated its sesquicentennial and chose to give special honors to a few outstanding professors among its faculty. Chia-Shun was given the title of Stephen P. Timoshenko Distinguished University Professor of Fluid Mechanics. In 1970 he was elected a member of Academia Sinica. In 1980 he was elected a member of the U.S. National Academy of Engineering. He was honored by the Chinese Institute of Engineers with the 1968 Achievement Award and by the Chinese Engineers and Scientists Association of Southern California with the 1973 Achievement Award. In 1974 he was the University of Michigan's Henry Russel Lecturer. In 1981 he was given the Theodore von Kármán Medal by the American Society of Civil Engineers. The American Physical Society gave him the Fluid-Dynamics Prize in 1985 and the Otto Laporte Award in 1989. In 1992 he had the honor to present the Sir Geoffrey Taylor Lecture at the University of Florida. Chia-Shun was a great admirer of Sir Geoffrey. Earlier, in 1976, Chia-Shun had dedicated to Sir Geoffrey a volume of *Advances in Applied Mechanics* that he edited. In the preface, Chia-Shun said of G. I. Taylor, "His work was always marked by an originality of thought and a freshness of approach that continue to delight his readers, and a characteristic welding of analysis to experiments that is rarely attempted, let alone attained, by others." My feeling is that this describes Chia-Shun himself very well.

In daily life the Yih family is warm, relaxed, and somewhat idealistic. Son Yiu Yo is a computer expert, son David is a Ph.D. musician, and daughter Katherine is an ecological biologist working on public health. Chia-Shun played flute and painted with oils in the style of the French impressionists. He was gregarious and a wonderful storyteller. He loved to eat and often cooked for friends. He was a true gardener and could name many plants by their Latin names. He took long walks in the countryside everyday whenever weather permitted. He loved students and treated them as family members. Inspiration could come to him at any time, in any place. During the garden wedding ceremony of his daughter, he whispered to me that he had suddenly found the solution of a solitary wave.

Chia-Shun enjoyed good health all his life. Two days before his death, he planted five young flowering trees in his garden. Friends watching him digging the holes asked him, why he must dig the holes so big and so deep? He answered, "At my age, I want to make sure that every sapling gets its full share of endowment! None should be shortchanged." On April 24, 1997, Chia-Shun died while on a commercial airline flight from Detroit to Taipei to participate in the Conference on Mechanics and Modern Science at the Academia Sinica. When a stewardess tried to wake him up for a stop at Tokyo, she found him unconscious. The passenger sitting next to Chia-Shun said he did not notice Chia-Shun had any signs of discomfort. Chia-Shun was sent to a hospital immediately after landing, but he never woke up. That was April 25th in Tokyo, the 24th in Detroit.

Chia-Shun's lighted cigarette study found more formal presentations in his Ph.D. dissertation and in his first two papers: one in the *Journal of Applied Mechanics* (1950) under the title of "Temperature Distribution in a Steady, Laminar, Preheated Air Jet," and another in the *Proceedings of the First U.S. National Congress of Applied Mechanics (1950)* under the title of "Free Convection Due to a Point Source of Heat." His formulation of the problem and his solutions were really elegant. The laminar flow solution was exact, and it was accompanied by a systematic experimental investigation on the transition from laminar to turbulent flow. These studies were followed by a series of papers dealing with atmospheric diffusion, gravitational convection from a boundary source, turbulent buoyant plumes, buoyant plumes in a transverse wind, etc. His characteristic approach was to find exact solutions as far as possible, and to check with experimental results. From his first paper to the one hundred thirtieth, the spirit was the same.

Chia-Shun's scientific papers published between 1950 and the early part of 1990 have been collected in a two-volume set called *Selected Papers by Chia-Shun Yih,* published by World Scientific, Singapore, 1991. It contains ninety-seven articles divided into five categories: (1) stratified flows and internal waves, (2) theory of hydrodynamic stability, (3) gravity waves, (4) jets, plumes, and diffusion, and (5) general. Chia-Shun's papers that appeared in the period from 1990 to 1997, after the publication of the *Selected Papers,* are listed at the end of this memoir. These include his theories of (a) colliding solitons, (b) infinitely many superposable solutions of the Navier-Stokes equations, and (c) added masses: the kinetic energy mass, momentum mass, and drift mass in steady irrotational subsonic flows, and in periodic water waves and sound waves, and (d) his theory of the instability due to viscosity stratification. A brief summary follows:

The first category, stratified flows and internal waves, is uniquely Yih's. A celebrated Yih transformation is used to simplify the mathematics. This transformation was announced in his paper "On the Flow of a Stratified Fluid" (Proceedings of the Third U.S. National Congress Applied Machanics) 1958, pages 857-861. He used a transformed stream function ψ' defined as:

$$\sqrt{\rho}\; u = \partial\psi' / \partial z, \; \sqrt{\rho}\; w = -\partial\psi' / \partial x,$$

where (u,w) are the components of velocity in the (x,z) directions, and p is the density. He showed that the governing equation for the stream function ψ' is:

$$\nabla^2\psi' + (gz/\rho_0)\, d\rho / d\psi' = (1/\rho_0)\, dH/\partial\psi',$$

in which g is the acceleration of gravity, ρ_0 is a reference density, and H is the total head. H is a constant along a streamline, and therefore a function of ψ' only. If $d\rho/d\psi'$ and $dH/d\psi'$ are linear in ψ', then the solutions of the linear governing equation yield exact solutions to large-amplitude motions. Similar transformations have also been given by him for a compressible fluid. The three-dimensional case is accomplished by the mapping $(u,v,w) = \lambda(\rho)\, (U,V,W)$, where (u,v,w) and (U,V,W) are the three components of velocity and $\lambda(\rho)$ is a function of the density, ρ.

The interplay of density stratification and gravitational force gives rise to a variety of interesting natural phenomena. Yih solved problems on the hydraulic jump of layered fluid, atmospheric phenomena, flow in porous media, prevention of stagnation zones in flows of a stratified or rotating fluid, edge waves, vortex rings, internal waves in pipes, similarity of stratified flows, instability driven by viscosity stratification, subharmonic instabilities in modulated viscous flows, long wave analysis of free-surface instabilities, surface-tension modulated waves, etc.

The second category of Yih's papers on the theory of hydrodynamic stability consists of a series of fundamental papers on two-dimensional parallel flow for three-dimensional disturbances, the stability of unsteady flows or configurations, eigenvalue bounds for the Orr-Sommerfeld equation, electrically conducting fluids, non-Newtonian fluids, viscosity stratification, and thermal conductivity stratification. This series of basic papers includes his solutions of a number of aeronautical, civil, and manufacturing engineering problems. Examples include the flow down an inclined plane, the waves in the deicing liquid sprayed on an airplane wing to deice the plane in cold winter weather, and waves in the sheet of paper pulp spread on a rotating cylinder in the process of paper making.

The third category of Yih's work is gravity waves. He gave solutions to water waves in basins of variable depth, waves in channels of various cross sections, waves in meandering rivers, edge waves created by a long-shore current and a ridge in the seabed, nonlinear wave groups, and ship waves.

Papers in the fourth category on jets, plumes, and diffusion are especially relevant to environmental concerns. Lighted cigarettes, chimneys, and polluting cities have a lot in common.

Finally, a large number of Yih papers collectively classified as the general category exhibit the breadth of his interest, from pure mathematics to magnetohydrodynamics and biomechanics. Altogether, the *Selected Papers by Chia-Shun Yih* preserves a good record of his journal articles.

In addition, Yih published two books on stratified flows and one on the whole field of fluid mechanics. His *Dynamics of Nonhomogeneous Fluids* was published by Macmillan in 1965. The second edition of this book, which contains a great deal of new material, was given a new title, *Stratified Flows* (Academic Press, 1980). The Yih style of fresh and concise writing shines through. This style is particularly evident in his third book, *Fluid Mechanics, A Concise Introduction to the Theory* (McGraw Hill, 1969). When this book went out of print in 1979, Chia-Shun issued an improved edition through the West River Press in order to reduce its price for the benefit of students.

Chia-Shun was interested in biomechanics also. In 1968 he and I published a paper together, entitled "Peristaltic Transport" (*Journal of Applied Mechanics*, 1968, pages 669–675). We were aiming to understand a disease called hydroureter, in which the ureter becomes enlarged, the peristaltic transport becomes ineffective, and the kidney injured.

Chia-Shun did not work much further on biological problems. But he laid out a plan to study the blood flow in large arteries by means of the Orr-Sommerfeld equation. When he solved the colliding soliton problem in 1993, we discussed extensively to aim further research on the arterial blood flow problem. There is no doubt that solitons can exist in arteries because of the nonlinear characteristics of the elasticity of the blood vessel wall, which stiffens as the strain increases. But the arterial tree is characterized by its branching pattern, each branch is not very long, and the flow is characterized by the forward and reflected waves. Hence his colliding solitons theory is relevant. Unfortunately, he died too soon.

Chia-Shun's last manuscript was entitled "Tornado-like Flows." One day, after a long drive from Gainesville, Florida, to Ann Arbor, Michigan, he called me to tell me that he and Shirley had arrived home safely; and that while Shirley was driving, he found a mathematical model of a tornado. He added to a swirling horizontal flow of a fluid a core of another fluid of different density and temperature, and a model of a tornado is obtained. In his head, he worked out the mathematical facets of how a core can lead the weather condition at a high altitude to the ground, how the horizontal swirling will generate the maximum speed at the surface of the core at the ground level, how the cyclonic action would cause the tornado to spin counterclockwise looking down toward the earth in the northern hemisphere, but clockwise in the southern hemisphere, and how sometimes a λ shaped tornado can be formed. He explains why the debris of a tornado is always thrown to the left in the northern hemisphere. It remained only to check the literature, ask the experts about the facts, do some numerical calculations, and write it up. I have a rough draft of the paper, but I have not succeeded in tracking down its publication.

The *Selected Papers by Chia-Shun Yih* includes only his mathematical and physical articles. His other writings were omitted. I am glad that his "Remembrance of G.I. Taylor" remained in the *Selected Papers* (pages 1005–1009). But I wish you could read his literary piece, "Old China Remembered," published in *The Ohio Review* 18 (1977), pages 67–77, (Bibliography No. 84, *Selected Papers*, page 1020). It consists of five short stories, entitled "The Slate Court," "Crepuschule," "Mulberries," "Silk from Wild Cocoons," and "Winter-Sweet." Through them we would really understand the life and imaginations of young Chia-Shun. Donald Hall, the poet, in his introduction to this article, said, "When I think of Chia-Shun now in his absence, he smiles with a wild enthusiasm—and it may be enthusiasm over a poem a thousand years old, or over a problem he is solving, or over the petal of a flower in front of us. He delights in the . . . but unlike most humans—scientist or poet or salesman or factory worker— his world moves far outside the borders of his work; it is wide with things to be loved and cherished."

An illustration of Chia-Shun's seeing poetry in fluid mechanics and fluid mechanics in poetry can be found in the frontispieces of his books. He chose a 1946 photograph of a wheat field in western Kansas to illustrate the dynamics of nonhomogeneous fluids and a thirteenth century Chinese painting of a tidal bore to illustrate fluid mechanics, and he quoted the poems of La Fontaine, Li Chong Chu, and Fung Yen Ci to introduce various topics in fluid mechanics. Such a poetic mind was his!

A list of Yih's papers published before 1990 is given in *Selected Papers by Chia-Shun Yih*. Those published from 1990 to 1997 are presented below.

Yih, C.S. 1990. "Wave Formation on a Liquid Layer for Deicing Airplane Wings." *Journal of Fluid Mechanics*, 212: 41–53.

Yih, C.S. 1990. "Infinitely Many Superposable Solutions of the Navier-Stokes Equations: Damped Beltrami Flows." In *Of Fluid Mechanics and Related Matters*, proceedings of a symposium honoring John Miles on his 70th birthday, December 1990.

Yih, C.S. 1993. "General Solution for Interaction of Solitary Waves Including Head-on Collisions." *Acta Mech. Sinica* 9:97–101, Science Press, Beijing.

Yih, C.S. 1993. "Solitary Waves in Stratified Fluids and Their Interaction." *Acta Mech. Sinica* 9:193–209, Science Press, Beijing.

Yih, C.S. 1994. "Solitary Waves in Poiseuille Flow of a Rotating Fluid." *Quarterly of Applied Mathematics*, 52:739–752.

Yih, C.S. 1994. "Intermodal Interaction of Internal Solitary Waves." *Quarterly of Applied Mathematics*, 52:753–758.

Yih, C.S. 1995. "Kinetic-Energy Mass, Momentum Mass, and Drift Mass in Steady Irrotational Subsonic Flows." *Journal of Fluid Mechanics*, 297:29–36.

Yih, C.S. and Wu, T.Y-T. 1995. "General Solution for Interaction of Solitary Waves Including Head-On Collisions." *Acta Mech. Sinica* 11:193–199.

Yih, C.S. and Zhu, S. 1996. "Selective Withdrawal from Stratified Streams." *Journal of the Australian Mathematical Society, Series B* 38:26–40.

Yih, C.S. 1996. "Added Mass." *Chinese Journal of Mechanics,* 12:9–14.

Yih, C.S. 1997. "The Role of Drift Mass in the Kinetic Energy and Momentum of Periodic Water Waves and Sound Waves." *Journal of Fluid Mechanics,* 331:429–438.

Yih, C.S. 1997. "Evolution of Darwinian Drift." *Journal of Fluid Mechanics,* 347:1–11.

Charles A. Zraket

CHARLES A. ZRAKET

1924–1997

BY GERALD P. DINNEEN AND ROBERT R. EVERETT

C HARLES A. ZRAKET, retired chief executive officer of the MITRE Corporation, died in Boston, Massachusetts, on December 3, 1997. Charles A. Zraket, known to his many friends as Charlie or CAZ, was born on January 9, 1924, in Lawrence, Massachusetts. Charlie received all his education and did most of his work in Massachusetts. He received a B.S. degree (magna cum laude) in electrical engineering from Northeastern University in 1951 and the M.S. degree in electrical engineering (cum laude) from the Massachusetts Institute of Technology.

Charles A. Zraket is one of the pioneers in the field of information systems engineering who continued to expand his interests and contributions as the field developed and grew. Charlie was one of a small number of engineers working on the new digital computers in the early 1950s. In 1951, while still a student at MIT, Charlie joined the pioneering MIT Digital Computer Laboratory, beginning a career that spanned the revolutionary developments in digital computing hardware and software. As a member of the MIT group that built the Whirlwind computer (now in the Smithsonian Institution), he designed the hardware and software system that permitted the machine to accept real-time inputs, a truly groundbreaking effort at that time. When the MIT Lincoln Laboratory was formed, he served as a group leader in the Digital Computer Division until 1958. Without the operating systems common today, Charlie and his co-

workers at MIT Lincoln Laboratory designed and tested the
weapons direction and intercept guidance system for the prototype air defense system called the Cape Cod System. He led the
group responsible for design of the planned operational air defense system (SAGE) and the formulation of the operational
and mathematical specifications for the SAGE system. This experience contributed to the development of tools for software
development and provided an important forerunner for the large
software industry today.

In 1958 the development work at MIT Lincoln Laboratory
had demonstrated the feasibility of an air defense system using
the new technologies of digital computing, digital communications, and advanced radar in an integrated system, and the first
centers of the SAGE system were declared operational. Charlie
became one of the founding members of a new nonprofit company, named MITRE, spun off by MIT to carry on further developments in air defense and other computer-based military systems. At MITRE, Charlie's work on SAGE led to his involvement
in numerous other military systems employing communications,
command, control, and intelligence (C^3I). Always looking for
new challenges, Charlie founded the Civil Systems Division of
MITRE, which provided information systems engineering to civilian agencies such as the Federal Aviation Administration, the
National Aeronautics and Space Administration, and the Environmental Protection Agency. He became president and chief
executive officer of MITRE in 1986 and retired from MITRE in
1990.

Following his retirement, Charlie continued as a trustee of
MITRE and became a scholar-in-residence at the Center for Science and International Affairs of the Kennedy School of Government, Harvard University, served on the boards of several
not-for-profit and for-profit organizations, and was an active vol-
unteer with the National Academy of Engineering and the National Research Council.

Charlie transferred his experiences and wisdom through numerous advisory activities, including service with the Defense
Science Board; the Science, Technology, and Public Policy Program, Harvard University; the Center for Arms Control and In-

ternational Security, Stanford University; the Center for Naval Analysis; and the Hudson Institute.

Charlie Zraket was elected to the National Academy of Engineering in 1991. His citation reads, "For significant engineering contributions related to information systems and national defense." Charlie was a fellow of the American Academy of Arts and Sciences, the American Association for the Advancement of Science, the American Institute of Aeronautics and Astronautics, and the Institute of Electrical and Electronics Engineers. Charlie was also a member of engineering honor societies Tau Beta Pi, Eta Kappa Nu, and Sigma Xi.

For the National Academy of Engineering, he served on the 1997 Nominating Committee, the Committee on Membership (1995 to 1997), and the Special Fields and Interdisciplinary Engineering Peer Committee (1993 to 1996). His service for the National Research Council preceded his election to the NAE and continued afterward. He was a member of the Commission on Physical Sciences, Mathematics, and Applications and served on many committees. One of special importance was the Panel to Review Earth Observation System Distribution (EOSDIS) Plans (1992 to 1993), which he chaired, combining his systems engineering talent and his interest in the environment.

Charlie was awarded an honorary doctorate of engineering by his alma mater, Northeastern University, in 1988. He received the MIT Distinguished Corporate Leadership Award in 1985 and was awarded the Department of Defense Medal for Distinguished Public Service. He has also been awarded the American Institute of Aeronautics and Astronautics Reed Aeronautics Award for 1993 and the Air Traffic Control Association Medallion Award for outstanding contributions to the science of air traffic control.

Charlie was a hard worker with many interests and gave his time and energy to many people and organizations. Charlie was a "doer," one of his greatest characteristics. He was smart, street wise, energetic, and well organized. When he took responsibility for a job, and he took on many, the work was done well and promptly. As a result he was in great demand and had admirers around the world. He spoke and wrote often on both technical and policy matters and served on numerous boards, including

BankBoston, Emerson Hospital, the Computer Museum, and the Volvo advisory board. His many interests ranged from defense research and development through arms control to energy and environmental policy.

Despite his many public commitments, Charlie always had time for his wife and his four children as well as his extended family, which included his younger brothers and their families. Charlie was head of the clan and was never too busy to provide help and counsel. He enjoyed people and had many friends, ranging from Herman Kahn, the futurist, to Bob Berks, the sculptor. Kahn chose him for the board of his Hudson Institute while Berks presented him with a bronze likeness. Charlie enjoyed a lively debate with friends and coworkers, often over a dinner.

One of his great pleasures was golf, which he enjoyed wherever he happened to be. Charlie was a money player in golf as in life. He played best when the chips were down.

Only a few of his close friends knew all of his interests and accomplishments, but all of us will miss him and continue to regret that we did not know him better.

APPENDIX

Members	Elected	Born	Deceased
Frederic W. Albaugh	1978	April 17, 1913	February 22, 1999
Harvey O. Banks	1973	March 29, 1910	September 22, 1996
Melvin L. Baron	1978	February 27, 1927	March 5, 1997
Milo C. Bell	1968	June 4, 1905	April 21, 1998
J. Lewis Blackburn	1997	October 2, 1913	February 23, 1997
J. Keith Brimacombe	1997	December 7, 1943	December 16, 1997
Gordon S. Brown	1965	August 30, 1907	August 23, 1996
John D. Caplan	1973	March 5, 1926	April 27, 1998
Wallace L. Chadwick	1965	December 4, 1897	June 5, 1996
Julian D. Cole	1976	April 2, 1925	April 17, 1999
Alfred R. Cooper, Jr.	1996	January 1, 1924	December 13, 1996
Georges A. Deschamps	1978	October 18, 1911	June 20, 1998
J. Presper Eckert	1967	April 9, 1919	June 3, 1995
Howard W. Emmons	1965	August 30, 1912	November 20, 1998
Eugene G. Fubini	1966	April 19, 1913	August 5, 1997
Donald F. Galloway	1984	March 22, 1913	December 21, 1996
H. Joseph Gerber	1982	April 7, 1924	August 8, 1996
Edward L. Ginzton	1965	December 27, 1915	August 13, 1998
André Y. Giraud	1977	April 3, 1925	July 27, 1997
John V. N. Granger	1975	September 14, 1918	December 1, 1997
John E. Gray	1992	April 13, 1922	October 20, 1997
Richard W. Hamming	1980	February 11, 1915	January 7, 1998
N. Bruce Hannay	1974	February 9, 1921	June 2, 1996
Clair A. Hill	1992	April 20, 1909	April 11, 1998
Nicholas J. Hoff	1965	January 3, 1906	August 4, 1997
Hoyt C. Hottel	1974	January 15, 1903	August 18, 1998
George R. Irwin	1977	February 26, 1907	October 9, 1998
Burgess H. Jennings	1977	September 12, 1903	June 6, 1996
Robert A. Laudise	1980	September 2, 1930	August 20, 1998
Hans List	1989	April 30, 1896	September 10, 1996
Harvard Lomax	1987	April 18, 1922	May 1, 1999
Albert G. Mumma	1976	June 2, 1906	July 15, 1997
Ryoichi Nakagawa	1990	April 27, 1913	July 30, 1998
Kenneth D. Nichols	1968	November 13, 1907	February 21, 2000
Franklin F. Offner	1990	April 5, 1911	May 1, 1999
John R. Philip	1995	January 18, 1927	June 26, 1999
Otto H. Schmitt	1979	April 6, 1913	January 7, 1998
Judith A. Schwan	1982	April 16, 1925	March 19, 1996
Joseph F. Shea	1971	September 5, 1926	February 14, 1999
Robert S. Silver	1979	March 13, 1913	April 21, 1997
Werner Stumm	1991	October 8, 1924	April 14, 1999

continued on next page

283

Members	Elected	Born	Deceased
Victor G. Szebehely	1982	August 10, 1921	September 13, 1997
Hans J. P. von Ohain	1980	December 13, 1911	March 13, 1998
Elmer P. Wheaton	1967	August 15, 1909	December 28, 1997
Eugene C. Whitney	1986	August 26, 1913	March 22, 1998
Frank Whittle	1979	June 1, 1907	August 8, 1996
F. Karl Willenbrock	1975	July 19, 1920	August 24, 1995
Chia-Shun Yih	1980	July 25, 1918	April 25, 1997
Charles A. Zraket	1991	January 9, 1924	December 3, 1997

ACKNOWLEDGMENTS FOR THE PHOTOGRAPH

FREDERIC W. ALBAUGH, courtesy of PNL Photography, Richland, Washington

MILO C. BELL, by Images by Edy

JOHN D. CAPLAN, by Leo Knight Photography, Southfield, Michigan

EUGENE G. FUBINI, by Fabian Bachrach

JOHN E. GRAY, by Fabian Bachrach

HANS LIST, by Foto-Furgler, Graz, Austria

NICHOLAS J. HOFF, courtesy of the News and Public Service Office, Stanford University

BURGESS H. JENNINGS, by Nickerson, Evanston, Illinois

WERNER STUMM, courtesy of the Swiss Federal Institute of Technology

FRANK WHITTLE, courtesy of the Smithsonian Institution

CHIA-SHUN YIH, courtesy of the University Of Michigan

CHARLES A. ZRAKET, by Fabian Bachrach